Scarred by Struggle,
Transformed by Hope

Scarred by Struggle, Transformed by Hope

Joan D. Chittister

WILLIAM B. EERDMANS PUBLISHING COMPANY
GRAND RAPIDS, MICHIGAN / CAMBRIDGE, U.K.

© 2003 Wm. B. Eerdmans Publishing Co.

All rights reserved

Published 2003 by
Wm. B. Eerdmans Publishing Co.
2140 Oak Industrial Drive N.E., Grand Rapids, Michigan 49505 /
P.O. Box 163, Cambridge CB3 9PU U.K.

Paperback edition 2005

Printed in the United States of America

12 11   12 11

ISBN 978-0-8028-2974-0

www.eerdmans.com

This book is dedicated to my Benedictine Sisters in Erie
who have been with me in the struggle
and brought hope along the way.

Contents

Preface: Struggle, the Seedbed of Hope

This is the book I didn't want to write.

It is certainly the book I did not intend to write. My original plan was that I would write a book about hope. It is, after all, a particularly unpredictable and often difficult period in human existence. It seemed to me that hope is the central virtue in life, certainly needed and so easy to explain. But it didn't work. Everywhere I looked, hope existed — but only as some kind of green shoot in the midst of struggle. It was a theological concept, not a spiritual practice. Hope, I began to realize, was not a state of life. It was at best a gift of life.

I saw optimists everywhere, of course, but optimism didn't interest me. To be blissful in the midst of pain, to avoid bad news like the plague, it seemed to me, was no great indicator either of mental health or of spiritual depth. I knew of no scriptures anywhere that answered grief by pretending it didn't exist. Christianity, my own tradition, rooted its hope in the other side of the cross. But it never denied the cross. On the contrary.

I wanted to know why it was that some people came through struggle whole of heart and sure of soul. I wanted to know what was missing in the lives of those others who seemed to slog through life, sure only that tomorrow would be worse than yesterday.

The more I struggled with the idea of hope, the more I began to realize that it is almost impossible to write a real book about hope without looking at the nature of struggle. Where in pain does hope lie?

And how do we cultivate it? And what does that mean to the development of the spiritual life and the attainment of emotional wholeness?

Consequently I gave up the notion of writing a book about the theological dimensions of hope — which fine theologians had already done — and decided to concentrate instead on the relationship between struggle and hope. This, I think, is where most of us live every day of our lives and this is where we do or do not live "the spiritual life." I wanted to deal with the real, the immediate, the present, and the obvious. But where could I go to discover that, to see it in action, to measure the truth of it by the truth of my own life?

Everybody in the world — including you and me — has stories of pain and grief, depression and despair, hopelessness and sorrow. Some of them we survived well. Some of them we didn't. The question is, *why?*

When struggle comes, as struggle does to every life, it's never easy to go on. It often seems that not going on at all would be the better thing. The easier thing. The only possible thing. Pressures from outside us, pressures from within, hang heavy on our shoulders, weigh us down, and dampen our hearts. Then the spirit is taxed beyond belief. Then all the pious little nosegays we've ever learned turn to sand. Then we begin to question: What is the use of all this pain? What is the purpose of all this struggle? How can anyone possibly make sense of such unremitting heartache? What good is hope in the face of a life marked over and over again by the ravages of despair? And yet we sense that the way we deal with struggle has something to do with the very measure of the self, with the whole issue of what it is to be a spiritual person.

Every major spiritual revelation known to humankind, in fact, is based on the bedrock of hope. Hinduism sees life as the gathering of graces that leads, eventually, to the eternal dissolution of each of us into the energy that is God. Buddhism teaches the path to Enlightenment, to the end of suffering. Judaism lives in the life-giving law of God and waits for the Messiah who will turn an unjust world into the eternal glory of God. Christianity embraces the Paschal Mystery and its movement from death to life through the crucifixion, death, and resurrection of Jesus Christ. Islam awaits the transformation from the physical burdens of this life to the spiritual freedom that comes with submission to God. Embedded in each is a spirituality of hope that imbues their followers with the power to believe in life, to cope with life, to live life, whatever the burdens that come with the daily dyings of life. But what is it? And what does it look like? And how do we access it when we need it ourselves? The answer, I think, lies in the stories of struggle and hope that each of these great traditions preserves.

Because all of us have stories of struggle and the ways it has affected us, this book is based on two stories as well: the ancient Judeo-Christian story of Jacob's wrestling match with the angel, and mine of an internal battle with life-changing disappointment. Through Jacob's story I began to understand both the cycle of struggle and the seeds of hope that had sprung out of them in my own life. I offer these stories, then, to help readers analyze their own stories of pain and despair, of hope and resurrection. Even more, they are meant to reveal the gifts that struggle can give to us all. By the time I had laid my own story against that of Jacob and the angel, I knew that hope and struggle were of a piece. I knew, too, that hope is built into struggle. Most of all, I knew that I had written the right book — at least for me.

This book is not a self-help manual. It is not a series of "steps" to anything. It is, rather, an anatomy of struggle and an account of the way hope grows within us, despite our moments of darkness, regardless of our regular bouts of depression. It is an invitation to look again at the struggles of life in order that we might remember how to recognize new life in our souls the next time our hearts turn again to clay, as turn they surely will.

Acknowledgments

⬧

The idea for this book came out of discussions about a book that, in the end, never came to be. The oil painter Samuel Bak is an artist whose work has great depth and soul-striking symbolism. I have been fascinated by his oil paintings for years. They astound me with their power. The original plan was that I would write with those particular works in mind.

Samuel Bak is a Holocaust survivor whose works over and over again record the obscenity, the tragedy, the eternally recurring reminder to us of both the depravity of the Holocaust and the nobility of humanity. The ovens of the Nazi death camps are a recurring theme in these works. Time is a shattered figure in these renderings. Yet, the odd thing, some would say, is that Samuel Bak does not consider himself to be a "Holocaust artist." Just as often as the ovens dominate one of his canvasses, just that often a long line of rabbis bridge the shattered gulf between the past and the present to make the old new again, to demonstrate the resiliency of the human spirit, to prove the irrepressibility of human truth. In every piece, a ladder tops the crematorium walls, or a green leaf sprouts, or the sun goes on shining in the midst of chaos. There was indeed a truth here that transcended, and at the same time, illuminated the private desperations of all our lives.

Obviously I did not, in the end, write about Sam Bak but I did write about what Sam Bak paints about: the emergence of hope as a facet, a heart-beat, a by-product of struggle for each of us, everywhere, through all time. I acknowledge Sam Bak and his work as proof of what this book seeks to analyze and lay bare: the umbilical cord between struggle and hope.

At the same time, and as echo of it, I acknowledge more than that. Books grow out of the lives of the people who write them, of course. But they also grow out of the lives of the people they touch. The writer writes one truth; the reader brings to it another. When we read something that has meaning to us, we ourselves give it a meaning it never had before. If what we read resonates with nothing we ourselves know to be true, we call it fantasy.

I wanted to know whether the model of suffering and hope that unfolds in these pages, that comes out of my own professional experience, out of my own personal life, in fact, spoke of the universally true. I wanted to know if the cycle of suffering as I have seen it and lived it and analyzed it and struggled with it over the years was recognizable to people I myself respected.

So I chose people whose capacity for truth I knew to be sound and asked them to read it. All of them are professionals. All of them have lived life well. All of them have lived through those moments in life that test us to the core. Many of them are themselves counselors and spiritual leaders. It is their authority I bring to the truth of this work as well as any understandings of mine.

The inadequacies in the text belong only to me, of course. But the confirmation of these insights is theirs.

I am grateful for the time they gave to this work. I am more than grateful for the experiences and ideas they shared with me that made it stronger than it would have been without them. I am deeply grateful for the quality of their comments. They are public figures, monastics, mental health professionals, theologians, writers, researchers, teachers, spiritual leaders, and professional colleagues. They are, most of all, human beings who know the truth of the way and the price of the path. I am grateful to Rosemary Haughton, Sr. Mary Lou Kownacki, OSB, Dr. Gail Freyne, Dr. Mary Claire Kennedy, SSJ, Dr. Vivian Lamberello, Dr. Judy Lynch, Dr. John Perito, Dr. Mary Hembrow Snyder, Jerry Trambley, Kathleen Stephens, Sr. Ann McCarthy, OSB, Sr. Linda Romey, OSB, Sr. Mary Miller, OSB, and Brother Thomas Bezanson for the wealth of spiritual wisdom and understanding each of them brought to this book. Each of these people brought more than wisdom to the task. They brought encouragement as well — the quality most at premium when a work bogs down in a writer's mind, loses its direction, and no longer seems worth its while.

As much as I am grateful to the readers of this manuscript, I am equally grateful to those generous friends — Mig Boyle, Gail Freyne, and Bill and Betsy Vorsheck — who provided the space, the distance, and the solitude that made possible the soul-searching that is basic to the writing of such a book as this. From the snow, the sea, and the mountains in which they immersed me, I received a great deal more than I was able to give in the process.

I am grateful, too, for the editing, research, and technical work of Sr. Marlene Bertke and Dr. Mary Lee Farrell, GNSH, that brought this book to completion.

Sandra De Groot, my project editor, is also my best prod and most patient companion. Sandra saw the idea for this book rise and fall several times in the process, proof that struggle is real and transformation is possible. But she never lost hope — or dampened mine.

Andrew Hoogheem, editor, worked gently with the text and allowed it to breathe on its own.

Finally, Sr. Maureen Tobin, long-time personal assistant and general all-round wisdom figure, suffered herself through one more of my struggles, made it seem possible, and held the world at bay as this book came to life.

Most interesting of all, perhaps, is the fact that if it weren't for the fact that the artist Sam Bak and the gallery owner, Bernie Pucker, were themselves the inspiration for this topic, it is possible that this book would never have been written. For that I am forever in their due.

For all these people, all these services of the soul, I am more grateful than words can ever say. They have all been present to me in more struggles than this and prove the power of the process.

1. A Paradigm of Struggle

L ife is a series of lessons, some of them obvious, some of them not. We learn as we go that dreams end, that plans get changed, that promises get broken, that our idols can disappoint us. We learn that there is such a thing as human support and that there is also such a thing as paralyzing isolation. We learn that life is a balancing act lived between the poles of unreasonable hope on one hand and disheartening disquiet on the other. We learn these things but we do not always understand them.

One thing time has taught me that can be learned no other way. One thing I know out of my own experience, despite years of wanting to deny it: However hard I strive to prove it otherwise, I know that there is no such thing as life without struggle. I have met it, indeed, from one end of life to the other. Over and over again, the foundations of life have shifted and slid away from me, sometimes changing the mental landscape only a little, other times shattering every given I've ever assumed into a kaleidoscope of pain. I have come through the death of loved ones, debilitating illness, life-shaping disappointment, and rejection by the very institutions and people that have meant the most to me. I lost a parent at an early age, lived in the tension of a "mixed marriage" at a time when the Catholic Church condemned such partnerships, grappled with the effects of teenage polio, dealt with the loss of my life's great ambition, and faced the possibility that I might be condemned publicly for questioning both the military policies of my country and the eucharistic theology of my church.

But those things are not the point of this book. The deeper truth with which this book attempts to deal is that my life is not an unusual one. There is no one, not anyone, who escapes the soul-wrenching experiences that stretch the mind but threaten to calcify the spirit.

There is no one who does not go down into the darkness where the waters do not flow and we starve for want of hope. Then life goes out of life and there is nothing left to do but simply follow routine, hoping down deep that we will not really have to go on much longer. It is a sad and barren time.

There is no one who does not have to choose sometime, someway, between giving up and growing stronger as they go along. And yet if we give up in the midst of struggle, we never find out what the struggle would have given us in the end. If we decide to endure it to the end, we come out of it changed by the doing of it. It is a risk of mammoth proportions. We dare the development of the self.

Life forges us in struggle. From one end of life to another we duel and joust, contest and dispute, rebel and revolt — against forces outside ourselves, yes, but against tensions within us as well. We struggle from infancy in an attempt to exert our own will on the world around us only to discover that we are pinioned in our efforts by the equally strong wills of those around us. We find ourselves pitted against forces of our own making and against forces beyond the edges of our understanding, greater than the limits of our strength to repel.

There is no one who has not known what it is to lose in the game of life, to feel defeat, to know humiliation, to be left standing naked and alone before the cold and staring eyes of a world that does not grieve for your grief. Everyone I know has driven back great waves of pain, weathered deep ruptures of life's innocent designs. I have a friend who is a Holocaust survivor, who as a Jewish boy was saved by Catholic nuns in the basement of their monastery. I know a woman who lived with incest all her young life, battered in body of course, but, worse, shattered in her own sense of self because of it. I know young children who were intimidated, beaten, and then thrown out of their homes in their grade school years, physically, brutally, by one after another of their mother's new boyfriends. I know a woman abandoned overnight by the perfect husband in the perfect marriage and left to struggle for her sanity. I have a friend whose beloved wife dropped dead, leaving him with five children under the age of twelve and taking half his very soul with her.

Indeed, I have seen person after person broken by the breaking open of life's great fissures. And I have also seen them survive. I have learned through them that all struggle is not destructive. I have come to understand from them that it is not struggle that defeats us, it is our failure to struggle that depletes the human spirit.

Something else I have come to know in them as well as in myself: All struggle is not loss. All those who struggle do not give way to depression, to death of the spirit, to dearth of heart. We not only can survive struggle but, it seems, we are meant to survive in new ways, with new insights, with new heart.

Struggle is part of life. In fact, struggle is an unavoidable part of life. It comes with birth and it takes its toll at every stage of development. In each of them we strive for something new at the price of something gained. We tussle between the dark and the daylight moments of the soul. If we stop struggling, we may die. But if we struggle and lose, we stand to die as well. So how are we to think of struggle? Is it loss or is it gain?

Life itself is the answer. If no one can escape struggle, then it must serve some purpose in life. It is a function of the spirit. It is an organic part of the adventure of development that comes only through the soul-stretching process of struggle. No other dimension of life can possibly offer it because no other process in life requires so much so deeply of us. Struggle bores down into the deepest part of the human soul like cirrus tendrils, bringing new life, contravening old truisms. The problem is that struggle requires the most of us just when we expect it least.

I remember one great life-changing moment of my own life very well. In fact, I live with it still. I was about twenty-eight years old when it happened, just young enough to think that anything was possible, just old enough to begin to realize that time was at a premium. From the age of fourteen, I had known myself to be a writer. It was an unshaped, inchoate, amateurish knowing — but a knowing nevertheless. Since second grade I had been making up plays for the rest of the neighborhood to present. I would probably have wound up playing a church organ someplace or honky-tonk piano in a music store if it had not been for the certain instincts of my first high school English teacher. It was my first week in secondary school and a particularly important day. That night I would be trying out for the basketball team. I'd been a short center on a losing grade school team, but there's a time in life when facts don't count much in either decisions or dreams. The dream of a high school career in basketball loomed large. In the course of that morning, however, I got called out of a freshman algebra class. The English teacher standing in the hall outside the classroom was holding a paper in her hand. She looked down at me with the piercing look nuns had when they were about to question your answers. No, I answered her, I had not copied my first essay assignment from anywhere; no, my parents had not written it for me; and yes, the idea for it was my own. "In that case," she said, the issue decided, "report to the journalism room immediately after school tonight." After that first night in the journalism room, I never thought of algebra or basketball ever again. I buried myself in the school newspaper. It became the whole reason for my existence, it seemed. Not basketball, not dances, not math or science. Unlike my friends, whose lives were filled with Friday night football games and summer days on the beach and weekends on the town, I stayed alone in the back of the old basement classroom and wrote.

I lived to write. I wrote all the time. I wrote in small notebooks and tiny date books and on sheets and sheets of blank white typing paper. I wrote half-sentences and long paragraphs, news stories and feature stories, editorials and humor columns. Then I waited for the newspaper to come out, to smell the ink, to touch the paper, to see the byline, to read and reread my own stories over and over again. But, secretly, I also wrote short story after short story after short story. These stories I never intended to show to anyone. They were my life within a life. I created characters and situations and places that said something to me about what I saw around me, about human struggle, about dark, driving motives and hidden pain. I never expected that anyone would ever read them. I simply wrote for the sheer joy of writing, the way some kids throw baseballs or practice the drums or swim laps in a pool.

Every day the situation became more and more clear: writing was all I wanted to do in life. At the same time, I had no idea how to go about doing it. Complicating the choice was the fact that I had wanted to be a nun even longer than I had wanted to be a writer. Conflict was built right into the situation. I had learned at a very early age that nuns were not writers. Nor, for that matter, were many other women. Once, alone in my high school library, I had scoured the shelves in search of books written by women. I found three: *Death Comes for the Archbishop* by Willa Cather; *Pride and Prejudice* by Jane Austen; and, miracle of miracles, a volume of poetry by "A Nun from Stanbrook." A nun. There was hope.

So I entered the monastery, still hugging the memory of those three orphaned volumes to my breast, still writing at every possible moment, a poem here, a journal entry there. All secretly. But the years went by with no writing to show for them except an essay for an educational journal here, a high school musical revue there. All of them routine parts of a teacher's tasks. Nothing of content. Nothing substantial. Nothing real. Instead, I was sent to teach double grades in a rural grade school and, eventually, history in secondary school. It was good work, teaching, but it was not the work that I knew to be me.

At the same time, religious life of that era was built almost entirely around the functional rather than the creative. We were educated to do what needed to be done. It was a no-frills approach to life. To ease the gap, perhaps, and, at the same time, to enable me to fit into a system that depended on a corps of interchangeable parts, I was allowed to major in English. The community needed English teachers and I liked working with words. It was second best but it was better than nothing. It was the closest I could get to literature, to real writing. It would equip me to teach English, of course, a function compatible with the then-concentration of religious in the Catholic school system, but my secret hope was that I would also learn to write by reading great writers.

I got a good, sound undergraduate program but it was still a cavernous distance from the world of creative writing that I felt drawing the flesh from my bones, sucking me in like a giant mystical vacuum buried beneath my ribs.

Then, suddenly, out of a black hole of nothingness it seemed to me, the word came from the prioress of my community, a woman given to strong and uncommon ideas, that now that the undergraduate degree was completed, I was to apply for admission to one of the greatest writing programs in one of the largest universities in the United States. I would begin study immediately for a master of fine arts degree in creative writing at Iowa State University. I remember that my hands shook as I signed the final registration papers, enclosed the writing sample, and sealed the large manila envelope. All this time, it finally seemed, the superiors of the community had known what I really wanted, where I really belonged, and it was going to happen. It was going to happen. Here. Monastery or no monastery. To me.

It was January when I received the letter of admission. I would begin the two-year program in June.

I don't remember much else about the rest of that year except that every day was suddenly easier than it had ever been before, every moment was light. It would all soon be over. I could afford to treat the dailyness of grades and papers and class periods lovingly. I could certainly give it my all for just a little while longer. As wrong as it had felt for years, there was suddenly no burden to it at all. Just finality. Just conclusion. Just gratitude. I had learned a great deal by teaching. I had figured out how to go on doing what I did not really want to do with some degree of grace. And I now knew gratitude for being able to move on, to become what I already knew myself to be. The future felt like gold and silver, looked like bright fuchsia and yellow sunflowers, smelled soft as lavender and warm as rye. I had never been happier in my life.

The school year went by in a blur. Mid-May came before I even realized that it was spring. And then, out of nowhere, I got another phone call. No explanation for it was ever given. To this day, I have no idea what lay behind the decision, what initiated the move, what caused the problem, what wrong I'd done. All I know is that the purpose of this call, from the very superior who had told me to make the application, was to tell me that I was to withdraw it, that it "would be better for my humility to go to our summer camp as third cook than to go to school." I was not, she said, "ready for a Master's degree."

And so began one of the greatest struggles of my life. Sometimes I wonder whether it's completely over yet. Most of all, I now wonder how I could ever have come to be the person I was meant to be if I had ever become the writer I thought Iowa State would make me.

That situation, my situation, would probably be meaningless to most people, trivial even — silly, perhaps — to many. There are few people who really care that much about writing. There may be even fewer now who give that much weight to being certified in one particular field. You can write, of course, without having an advanced degree in creative writing. There are many, I'm sure, who would actually find it good to be sent to a children's camp for the summer. In fact, for many people all those things — cooking at a children's camp without ever having to write a thing — would be a relief. But personal preferences are not the point. The point is that the situation was life-altering to me. It was cataclysm in the midst of calm. It was the end of the dream, the loss of the hope. It was forced change at the center of my personal universe. It was impossible. "Change that is real is change that is not willed," the holy one says.[1] For me, this was real.

Indeed, that particular situation was particular only to me and important to few, I'm sure. But disappointment is universal. Life-wrenching disappointment, soul-searing loss, everybody understands. Everybody sometimes in life is changed by something they did not want to have change. It is real change, the change that comes upon us unbidden and unwanted, change that breaks our hearts and smothers our souls and haunts us all. The divorce we do not want, the family scars we cannot face, the personal humiliations we cannot endure, the community catastrophes we could not avert and cannot undo leave us hollow to the core.

How do we explain such things? How do we bear them? How do we survive them? And most of all, what happens to us — spiritually — as a result?

---

1. Anthony de Mello, *One Minute Wisdom* (1988).

2. The Loss of Certainty: A Suffering of the Soul

❧

I am writing this book because struggle, long a recognized factor in personal development and spiritual growth, has become one of the major spiritual *problems* of our time. Change — the shifting of life from one stable context to another — envelops us. Nothing seems fixed anymore — not theology, not culture, not institutions, not relationships, not family, not even my own sense of self. In the postmodern world, with its critique of the modernist belief in progress, suspicion becomes the lens through which we view everything. We ask new questions: Is the church given to holiness or only to ritual? Is the West really creative or only exploitative? Are the poor really oppressed or only lazy? Is anything what it seems to be or does it all need to be deconstructed in order to raise up something purer in its stead? It begs a veritable philosophy of transition.

But like most people I was raised on absolutes and categories, on rules and certainties. I was told that my destiny was in my hands. If I worked hard, I would succeed. If I lived a good life, I would be rewarded. If I prayed hard enough, worked long enough, lived a regulated enough life, God would help me and guide me and work life in my favor. But the absolutes faded, the rules changed, even my image of God became bigger than the little, tribal, national, male idol who cared only for white North Americans. Now, I have come to see, little if anything is expected to last.

All the givens have changed and all the rules with them. Built-in obsolescence is the new given. Things are made to be discarded or up-graded or replaced. Everything in life is in flux. Everything in life is simply another step, not the final step, in the process of becoming something else. Life itself has become a series of life-changing inter-ruptions we are meant to expect and to broach with very little help. Life swirls around us and the people we count on go their own chang-ing ways.

Clearly we are living in an era more in need of a spirituality of struggle than perhaps any other time in history.

Never before in my lifetime has the entire universe, the social or-der, the sense of personal power, the promise of possibility, and even the surety of the spiritual life seemed so fragile. And all at the same time. The world is pregnant with uncertainty. In the last fifty years, the foundations of life, both personal and public, have pitched and rolled, canted and teetered between one claim and the next: this is the weapon to end all weapons, this is the diet to end all diets, this is the medicine to end all medicines, this is the culture that bests all cultures. "Nation-ality" is a thing of the past. National borders have simply ceased to ex-ist. We can live in virtual reality in any country of the world where a television camera or an Internet connection can go. We live in daily contact now with rivers of flesh-and-blood refugees who have been driven out of their homelands to the edges of ours in the face of drought or war, desertification or corporate encroachment. We watch them stream across the TV screens in our living rooms, dirty, hungry, and in despair. Civil wars and revolutions have redrawn the map of the world. Women are still bought and sold as sexual objects, domestic or otherwise. Small children are sold into slavery weekly. Destitution abounds in the richest period in human history. And all the while, the church itself is awash in tests of both its integrity and its theology as new findings put old answers to the question. Old values find them-selves facing new standards of judgment as science creates a world no church ever thought could possibly exist.

To resolve the tension that comes with ethical confusion, with po-litical conflict, with theologies of domination, some people cleave to the past even more tightly than before. Others put down the past en-tirely and take up little or nothing to take its place. But most of us sim-ply go on trying to find some point of meaning between the two. We want to hold on to what counts as well as to live in peace with whatever it is that comes into our lives.

Even spirituality and religion have become distinct entities as people continue to cling to one tradition but find themselves beginning to nourish it with the insights and comforts of many. Members of Generation X, the first generation of humankind brought up in a world of more religious pluralism than ethnic identity, grow up in one tradition but move effortlessly from one to another. Children from mixed families are raised in two churches; biracial adoption is commonplace; Christian families socialize with their Buddhist neighbors. Psychology, the study of individual development, has become a substitute for, or at least an addendum to, the Platonic notion of the absolute. The social propositions, the philosophical invariables, the religious dogmas upon which life was once thought to be unalterably grounded have gone to silt.

And through it all, each of us in our own private way has been brought face to face with the struggle that comes with every shift of social ground, every loosening of social certainties. The struggle between variables has become endemic. We find ourselves confronted with an experience of humanity, a sense of personal uprootedness, that we have never known before. Small-town life with its guarantee of the predictable is over. In its place are anonymity and traffic and bedroom communities rather than neighborhoods or farmlands. Globalization homogenizes the world and fragments it at the same time as groups struggle for place and identity in a world gone bland. Visitors to Manila hear American pop music in the airport concourse and read "Yankee, go home!" signs in the city. Militarism and fundamentalist terrorism stand eye-to-eye, each waiting for the other to blink. Fierce denominationalism has faded. In its place are mixed Bible-study groups and Muslim mosques and Hindu temples and courses in world religion in the most Catholic of cities, the most Protestant of places, the most Jewish of communities we know. The world is getting smaller, they tell us, but we know that it is also getting to be more than that. It is getting infinitely more confusing, infinitely more uncontrollable at the same time. We are now a people whose children are born in one state, educated in another, employed in a third, retired in a fourth, and buried in a fifth. We are people who wear clothes made in one nation, eat food grown in another, and work for someone who is a citizen of a third. We are people who travel the world and take it for granted. We are a globe on which some of the largest economies in the world are corporations, not nations. We are people born in a white, Western, Christian culture that we watch become more brown, more Eastern, more polyvalent every day.

It shakes us to the center of our souls.

The great new vision of the postwar period with its promises of peace, its vision of technological miracles, and its taste of economic security for everyone has given way to foul reality over and over again in the last fifty years. First we came face to face with the scope and the implications of the Holocaust. Then we came to realize the ultimacy of atomic warfare. Then we grappled with the shame of Vietnam. Then we watched the Doomsday Clock tremble closer and closer to the end-time of a Cold War. Then we counted the bodies left over by the methodical process of ethnic cleansing. Then we understood. There are no innocents anymore. There is no such thing as a noncombatant. We are all at risk.

We watched as they exposed for us the horrors of apartheid, the inhumanity of ethnic cleansing, the atrocity of sexism so deep that women were enslaved as "comfort-girls" and breeders of the next generation of military martyrs to whatever the male powers of the day might name to be worth the sacrifice. Finally we watched on the television sets in our living rooms as the center of Manhattan burned to the ground. We saw a small, anonymous band of extremist guerillas strike at the heart of the military-economic establishment of the United States by taking down the Twin Towers of New York's World Trade Center with no weapons at all save two of America's own commercial airliners. And as it toppled into dust, it took with it almost three thousand of our friends and family members, all taken down by an enemy we could not see and did not know. And in response to that murderous act, in the country from which they sprang or which harbored them, we killed twice as many innocents as they had managed to kill of us. Small comfort, surely. No gain, of course. Clearly humanity carried within itself, we were made to discover — forced to face — a depraved streak, even a vicious streak, perhaps. As a species, as nations, as peoples, as persons, we were all capable of the unthinkable. We were all doers of the undoable. We were all accessories to our own hubris.

These are not simply changes on the social landscape. These are not simply shifts in the social design of the day. These are issues that change our very understanding of ourselves, the very nature of many of our struggles. They change the shape of our lives. They challenge the fabric of our souls. They shake our certainties. They send us back upon ourselves for the unassailable direction the institutions are no longer able to give. In such a world, catechisms and Sunday school lessons, rituals and religious symbolisms take on new meaning, if as a matter of fact they take on any meaning at all. The whole question becomes, what, if anything, is there inside us to carry us through this period of social and personal disorientation, of social and personal malaise, of personal and social relativism, not just in order to make the confusion bearable but to vindicate the struggle?

At the same time, there is another side to this whirligig of swift social twists and harsh personal changes. There is the awareness of unlimited possibility, of certain growth, of life-giving change, both around us and within us. Life may feel precarious at times but life is also, we know, made up of a series of miracles. Love happens, relationships form, the job opens, the promotion comes, differences great and small melt into one another, we succeed in becoming just what we wanted to be.

We achieve and we acquire and we become and we finally find ourselves just where we want to be and life just the way we want to make it. And now things are perfect, we think. Now things are finally settled, whatever the shift in the sands under our feet. Now we are safe and in control and secure. And thinking that, of course, makes us least secure of all.

The illusion of benign unchangeability is a seductive one.

Each step along the way once accomplished, I have discovered, comes with a ring of permanence to it. But it isn't. It never is. It is always interrupted by an equally spectral series of obstacles and interruptions that make every next miracle seem impossible, every next point unreachable, every present situation unbearable. In the months before I began to write this book, I studied the geology of my own life with all its loops and curls, all its tortuous twists and dangerous turns. I saw a pattern emerge that I had never seen there before. I saw that life is a matrix of miracles punctuated by one interruption after the next.

Ironically enough, all of the miracles turn out to be dependent on the very interruption that threatened the existence of the miracle before it. If my father had not died, I would never have wound up in Erie, Pennsylvania. If I had never come to Erie, I would never have become a Benedictine. If I had never become a Benedictine, I would not be writing this book. I have come to understand what the poet Arthur O'Shaughnessy meant when he wrote, "Each age is a dream that is dying / or one that is coming to birth."[1]

The regularity of small and irritating, great and debilitating losses that threaten the death of the heart, that interrupt the flow of life are, I have discovered, of the essence of living. But that does not make them welcome guests. Just when we feel that we have finally gotten it right, finally achieved what we set out to get, finally found what we have always wanted, the bubble bursts, the bauble breaks, the future is gone. The spiritual question becomes how to go about each dying without giving in to the death of the soul. In that question lies the crux of a spirituality of struggle. In that question lies the difference between clinical depression and the angst of spiritual growth. For as many times as a person may be helped through the tremors of change by the soul-numbing drugs of psychiatry, there are just as many times that honest awareness, spiritual awareness, of the costs and challenges of change can do as well. There is a difference between mental pathology, those chemical imbalances of the mind, all of which call for drug therapy, and that standard-brand weariness of heart that takes the light out of life and the spark out of the soul. There is a difference between sick despair and those shocks of life that sour our laughter and gray our days, that turn the excitement of life into the burden of survival but which, if we understand them, do not, in the end, destroy us.

The great secret of life is how to survive struggle without succumbing to it, how to bear struggle without being defeated by it, how to come out of great struggle better than when we found ourselves in the midst of it. A spirituality of struggle exposes the secret to the world.

1. Arthur O'Shaughnessy, "Ode" (1874).

3. *Struggle: The Process and the Challenge*

∽

There are several ways to survive the interruptions of life. One way is to assume that what we don't want to have happen but can't change is God's mind for us — mysterious, but magical nevertheless. Another way is to endure what we can't change, however reluctantly, as a demonstration of some kind of vacuous virtue, the successful accomplishment of a great cosmic test that in the mysterious mathematics of the universe comes out to our credit.

We can, in other words, simply assume that life is a "plan" God makes for us. We see ourselves, in this view, as a collection of dancing puppets on a string, free within the range of the twine but captive to its latitudes. It is thus God the Puppeteer who becomes responsible for everything in life, not us. We are simply victims of God's designs. Whatever happens happens because God *wants* whatever perverted, malignant thing it is. Everything is always God's will: God's will that the poor are poor. God's will that women are routinely beaten and routinely ignored. God's will that lives are ruined and children abandoned and villages full of the helpless bombed out. God's will that my life is warped and broken and desperately unstable. God's will. This spirituality feeds the notion that God is responsible for evil — not we, not I. We human beings are simply pawns in God's great godless game.

At issue, in this case, is not how to handle struggle; at issue is faith. If we only had enough faith, we tell ourselves, we would accept the "will of God" for us and the hurt would not happen, the problem would not exist. We would embrace pain and in the embracing of it, turn it to pleasure. To think otherwise would make us deficient in virtue. What's wrong with me, I think, is not that I don't understand the gifts of struggle; what's wrong with me is some kind of primal and basic spiritual infidelity that keeps me from accepting what must be God's will.

There is a second way to deal with struggle, just as groundless, just as unhelpful as the first. We can assume that God is the Magician whose role it is to save us from the realities of life. God the Magician molds circumstances and consequences to our liking. This God makes red lights turn green so we're not inconvenienced at street corners and sees to it that death and suffering and pain become a kind of vending machine game. Put enough suffering in, get a blessing out. This is the "dancing is bad, drinking is bad, hemorrhoids are good" theology of life.

A spirituality of God the Magician makes life an exercise in spiritual huckstering. Everything, in this view, depends on being able to do some sort of soulful legerdemain that turns evil into good, acceptance of injustice into a lottery of rewards. All we need to do to be holy in this instance is to believe that pain is "better" for us here than happiness would be, that the more unhappy we are here, the happier we will be somewhere else. Then the rabbit will appear in the hat, the black silk scarf will turn to gold, the problem in the box will disappear.

From this perspective, the problem is not that we fail to see struggle as a stepping-stone to development. The problem is that we have not learned to anesthetize our feelings. The trick is to offer up the pain, accept the pain, and the pain will itself be good for us. But that is not a spirituality of struggle. That is an attempt to fool ourselves into thinking that we never wanted what we lost at all. It is an abject answer to the great losses of life and it never quite satisfies, never honors the past, and, at the same time, never completely becomes something new. Then we turn the process of struggle into a kind of spiritual masochism. If it hurts, we assume, it must be good for us.

In both approaches, what makes the victim a victim is that they have failed. Either they believe too little or they feel too much. Either they don't accept God's plan for them or they don't accept the fact that pain is good, unhappiness is better than happiness, defeat is better than victory.

But God is not a puppeteer and God is not a magic act. God is the ground of our being, the energy of life, the goodness out of which all things are intended to grow to fullness. Yet it is a struggle. How can we possibly equate the two — a good God with a life of tilts and jousts, of bad tries and great travail, the suffering of innocents and the hardship of failure? How can we possibly believe one term of the equation and at the same time understand the other? How can we possibly deal with the great erupting changes of life and come away more whole because of having been through them than we would possibly have been without them? To do that takes a spirituality of struggle that owns the pain but also comes to grips with each of its dimensions, with all of its demands. The spirituality of struggle is a process. It is, too, a catalyst and a series of gifts without which we cannot possibly become fully ourselves. But where can we go to trace the process and explore the gifts?

Every once in a while we get glimpses into the sundry elements, the complex core of the spirituality of struggle. We see it in the character of someone we know who has gone through it and been softened or strengthened or wizened by the doing of it. We recognize it in a piece of folklore that is suddenly confirmed by the truisms of our own lives. "No winter lasts forever," we say. "No spring skips its turn."[1] "While there is life there is hope,"[2] we remember. "Despair is the price one pays for setting an impossible aim,"[3] we remind ourselves. We recognize it, too, in the great wisdom stories of the past that raise for public reflection the great questions and insights garnered over time by those before us. They are stories that sharpen our own perceptions and shape our futures as well as tell us our past. They are everywhere, these narratives of hope. They emerge in every culture; they nest in the hearts of every people — in the Hindu story of Arjuna who struggles to discover the ethic above the ethic of warfare in the clan, in the Old English epic of Beowulf who defeats the dragon and saves the people, in the Jataka Tales of Buddhism and their models of the wisdom that

1. Hal Borland, "A Promise — April 29." *Sundial of the Seasons* (1964).
2. Marcus Tullius Cicero, *Epistolarum ad Atticum.*
3. Graham Greene, *The Heart of the Matter* (1948).

comes with endurance, in the Judeo-Christian story of Jacob who wrestles with God and emerges wounded but victorious. It is the Jacob story, I think, that best exposes the nature of struggle. It is the Jacob story that, when I look back, I recognize to have been at work in the major change points of my own life. It is the Jacob story, I know now, that became a template for understanding my own struggle to recover from the loss of the writing degree. Jacob and I — Jacob and you, perhaps — trod the same sad road of loss and isolation, darkness and fear, powerlessness and vulnerability, exhaustion and scarring. In the Jacob story are embedded all the dimensions of depression and despair — and all the seeds of growth and hope, as well. The story reads thus:

> That same night he rose, and taking his two wives and his two slave-girls and his eleven children he crossed the ford of the Jabbok. He took them and sent them across the stream and sent all his possessions over too. And Jacob was left alone.
>
> And there was one that wrestled with him until daybreak who, seeing that he could not master him, struck him in the socket of his hip, and Jacob's hip was dislocated as he wrestled with him. He said, "Let me go, for the day is breaking." But Jacob answered, "I will not let you go unless you bless me." He then asked, "What is your name?" "Jacob," he replied. He said, "Your name shall no longer be Jacob, but Israel. Because you have been strong against God, you shall prevail against men." Jacob then made this request, "I beg you, tell me your name," but he replied, "Why do you ask my name?" And he blessed him there.
>
> Jacob named the place Peniel, "Because I have seen God face to face," he said, "and I have survived." The sun rose as he left Peniel, limping because of his hip. (Genesis 32:22-32)

We shake our heads, mystified, at the telling of this story. It appears in the middle of the Genesis text, unprovoked and unclear. It appears out of nowhere and does nothing to advance the plot, it seems. It resolves nothing. And so we commonly ignore it. We consider it of very little importance. The best it does, it seems, is to raise great irritating questions in us: What is this scene doing here? What is it about?

Who is wrestling with Jacob? What are they wrestling about? Why is this happening now? What, if anything, can it possibly mean to me? The questions are legitimate.

It is an annoying little story, plucked out of nowhere, apparently, and wedged into the middle of a narrative about the rise and return of the heir triumphant. But I have an idea that in this story lies the whole stuff of struggle, the real process of change, the secrets of a spirituality of letting go and going on despite the pain, despite the extinction of what our heart tells us is the essential of our lives, struggle resolved, new gifts in hand.

The story is a simple one and, like many a life-changing event, comes along unexpected, unwanted, and unexplained. The Book of Genesis tells us that Jacob, son of Isaac, has made peace with Laban, his father-in-law, whose scheme to keep Jacob and his two daughters from returning to Jacob's own land has failed. Jacob is, moreover, on his way to reconcile with his brother Esau after years of hostility and separation. Life is good and getting better for Jacob. He is finally free of Laban's indentured servanthood. He is back in his own land. He has wives, and children, and cattle. He is comfortably well-off. And he is ready to take his father's place as head of the clan. Everything is resolved; everything is ready. One life is behind him and another one is about to begin. Then, that night, tired and alone, with no warning whatsoever that a struggle is about to begin, Jacob finds himself wrestling with the unknown, with a figure not of human origin — as we all do when we confront within ourselves either our demons or our God.

Just as the Jacob story seems to break the flow of the text, our own struggles begin at those junctures of life where the past disappears and the future seems both unclear and totally unacceptable. It is irreparable interruption. The loved one dies. The job fails. The money disappears. The promise is broken. The illness fells us. The marriage ends. The inner lights of life fizzle and dim, dullness sets in, and joy goes dry. In my own case, it was the unexplained and total dashing of all my academic plans to become a writer, the closing of a door without cause or care, the end of a dream that had been years in the making.

I saw in the Jacob story an archetype for my own struggle. As you read this book, you may discover that it is a paradigm for your story, too. And in thinking through both my story and Jacob's, you may see that struggle is not an isolated incident. Struggle is a process of pitfalls and challenges which, if met, become hope.

The situation is classic: It's not a matter of finding something difficult. It is a matter of feeling faced with the impossible. Just when we're least prepared we find ourselves lost to one world and unsure of the next. Just when it seems least likely, the great hiatus comes and life as we once knew it is ruptured forever. Just when good things seem more possible than they've been for a long, long time, perhaps, we're faced with the awareness that we stand to lose it all. Just when we are most vulnerable, just when we most want to let go, to give up, to quit, we find ourselves in the struggle of our lives, trying to survive, trying to go on. Why? Because going on is what life is all about. Because there is no other choice. The only question is whether we go on in the full of ourselves, or live wounded and dour for the rest of our lives. One way is depression; the other way is new life. One way is defeat; the other way is hope.

In the story of Jacob and the heavenly figure with whom he wrestles, we begin to see the elements of struggle and the unfolding, as well, of the nine gifts of spirit that go with them. Jacob faces change, isolation, darkness, fear, powerlessness, vulnerability, exhaustion, and scarring. They are, we see, the price to be paid for becoming new. To struggle is begin to see the world differently. It gives us a new sense of self. It tests all the faith in the goodness of God that we have ever professed. It requires an audacity we did not know we had. It demands a commitment to the truth. It leads to self-knowledge. It builds forbearance. It tests our purity of heart. It brings total metamorphosis of soul. If we are willing to persevere through the depths of struggle we can emerge with conversion, independence, faith, courage, surrender, self-acceptance, endurance, purity of heart, and a kind of personal growth that takes us beyond pain to understanding. Enduring struggle is the price to be paid for becoming everything we are meant to be in the world. What we see in these nine gifts are the shadows of hope that whisper around the edges of every pit in life. What we see is the fullness of the self come to birth the only way it really can: in labor and under trial.

4. The Struggle of Change

〜

The need to settle down, to get things right, plagues the human soul. It dogs us from one step to the next. We are not looking for excitement as we go through life nearly as much as we are seeking equilibrium, homeostasis, stability. We want to arrive. We want to get things under control. We want to achieve. We want to become the dream of our lives: to own the house or get the office or make the money or become the artist of something, maybe of anything. We want to sink into the marshmallow of life and enjoy what we have gained by the power of our hands or the cunning of our minds. We want the joy of looking back on the plains from which we've come to the mountaintop to which we've risen with a satisfied, if not a smug, smile. We want the rewards that come with hard work. We want to live in the new world we've created for ourselves, secure in its completion, safe in its bounties. We want to forget where we've come from, become what we aren't, count our flocks, and bury our gold. We want to be invulnerable in the moment we have created, whatever it takes to preserve it from the future. We have deserved it. We have achieved it. We all but own it. And we want it.

Achievement is a two-edged sword. It brings all manner of ghosts into play: a touch of smugness, great personal pride, a deep need for security. I don't want to lose what I've worked so hard all my life to build up. I want a little attention for having done what so many around me have not been able to do. Most of all, I want to be able to smile at the little kingdom I've created and warm myself in the glow of it. I deserve what I have done. No one has the right to take it away from me. I am finished now. I have finally gotten just what I wanted. I have become what I intended to be. It's mine. No one can touch it.

Here is where Jacob's story and my story begin to intersect. The feelings go deep. I remember all too well even now the terrible flash of anger, the numbing jolt of dismay that hissed in the center of my stomach like a steaming coal when that phone call came. Withdraw the application to the creative writing program? Impossible! I had waited all my life for it. I had been living for this minute for years. What was to be gained by ending what I had just been waiting to begin? Like Jacob, just when I thought my life was in order, I found myself suddenly at war. When the promised promotion does not come, when the one who said they would take care of us forever has the nerve to die or go away or love someone else, when life takes a sudden turn beyond our control, life stops and the flailing begins, both outside and in.

Struggle begins with shock. With loss. With radical interruption of what just minutes before had been certain and sure and drowsily eternal. It would never end. It could never end. My reputation could not end. My relationship could not end. My dreams could not end. But they do. And they did.

"Change means movement. Movement means friction."[1] So Saul Alinsky, the great social reformer, wrote. But movement is precisely what we do not want and friction is exactly what we cannot bear even to think about. When we have finally domesticated our lives, nothing must shift; nothing must change.

This great, gaping need to put down roots, to forestall the future for the sake of the present, to cement the eternal in the now, is one of life's greatest obstacles to the truth of the self. In cultivating only one part of myself, I may be dooming the rest of me to the desiccation of a living death. By clinging to the present I cut off the wings of the soul.

But change is the eternal constant. It comes, the psychologists tell us, at every stage of life for the sake of carrying us to the next one. It is biological and social, internal and external, of my own making and beyond my control.

1. Saul Alinsky, *Rules for Radicals* (1971).

When life changes under our feet, despite our resistance, without our permission, it is an invitation to growth. When I rail and balk at its changing, when I run and hide from the changes, when I struggle against the tides of life in order to cling to every earlier stage, it is a sure sign that I am not finished yet.

I can taste to this day the sick feeling that came with the phone call that would, in the end, change the entire direction of my life. I remember feeling tossed in the air like dry straw. I remember barely being able to breathe on the other end of the line. There went the short stories; there went the novels I would write. There went what I had wanted all my life. And all for no reason. All without cause. All without sense. And in its place, nothingness.

What I did not have that day was the wisdom of soul to ask what would come in their place? In fact, I had no patience for the thought of anything else. What I did not have that day was the strength of spirit to imagine that whatever the pain of the change, there was something in it that would call more out of me than I ever imagined was there.

"Every moment of one's existence," Norman Mailer wrote, "one is growing into more or retreating into less. One is always living a little more or dying a little bit,"[2] he said. The spirituality of struggle begins with the decision to grow or to retreat, to live a little more or to die a little bit. It is a decision of great import.

Some people get through it because, after the death, when the funeral is over, when the well-wishers have all gone back to their warm kitchens and welcoming beds, here in the silence there are children to be cared for, or unfinished work to be done in memory of the other. So, however empty, however lost, some move forward, captive to the demands of the past, and without even realizing it find themselves living into the future. "I had children," women say when they look back on their widowed years. "I had to go on." "Crippled or not, I had to support myself," the disabled say. "I wanted to finish what we had been working on when it happened," the survivors say. These are the lucky ones.

But for those for whom there is nothing left of the past and no rea-

2. Norman Mailer, *Conversations with Norman Mailer,* ed. J. Michael Lennon (1988).

son to bear the future, life can grow very cold, very mechanical. The body goes on but the spirit withers.

The traditional model of change — willed to the Western world by the Stoic philosophy of Greece, the patriarchal values system of Rome, and the ascetical tradition of Christianity — calls for the dogged endurance of pain. This is a "stiff upper lip" standard that represses hurt and sacrifices the self. It arises from male-dominated societies that measured the worth of a man by the amount of pain he could endure. In such cultures women, arbiters of the feelings of humankind, were simply left to wail their weakness away and endure. But with the loss of feelings comes the loss of the right to be human, to change, and to grow. The whole process of coming to wholeness through being willing to take the learnings of the past to the challenges of the present shrivels in the face of denial. In the traditional view, struggle required one of two things: that what could not be endured be changed or that what could not be changed be endured. Missing from the lexicon of options was the notion that we ourselves could do more than endure: we could be transformed by the possibility of new beginnings.

The essence of struggle is neither endurance nor denial. The essence of struggle is the decision to become new rather than simply to become older. It is the opportunity to grow either smaller or larger in the process.

There is, then, a gift hidden in the travails of forced change. It is the gift of beginning again: *conversion.*

5. The Gift of Conversion

⸎

The first gift of struggle is the call to conversion — the call to think differently about who God is and about who I am as an individual. It calls us to think again about what life really means and how I go about being in the world. These are deeply spiritual questions that touch on our notions of God as well as on our ideas of ourselves.

To the patriarchal mind-set God is mighty warrior, stern judge, law-giving father, under whose dominion all things fall. To grow spiritually in the image of this God is to be in control, to conquer what is unacceptable in us and around us. To dominate at all costs. To get what is our due.

There is very little give in a life bent on conquest. It is a psychological straitjacket, a spiritual dead end. Once I'm in control, either of me or of the world around me, I have neither the need nor the ability to continue growing.

But there is another way to think about God. To the newly retrieved feminist mindset of nearly every spiritual tradition, God is not only caring father but birthing mother as well, who brings new life with the rising of every sun and the descent of every inner darkness. To grow spiritually in the image of our mother God is to be open to newness, to expect surprise, to understand pain, to soothe hurt, to nurture difference rather than to deny it.

To live bent on conversion is to live welcoming of the tomorrow that is already in embryo, rather than to attempt to cement today into eternity. Conversion does not expect to settle down, it expects only to become new over and over again. It sees change as the impetus to explore the other part of the self, demanding as that may be to do, difficult as that may be to begin, unwanted as that may be at this time.

The kind of change that shocks us into new beginnings is the kind of change that gives us new life. Yes, it forces us down unwanted paths, leads us stumbling through the Mephistophelean rills and recesses of the dark sides of the soul — angry, fearful, resistant, and unbelieving. But it also prods us from task to task in life until, at the end, we find ourselves full-statured and full of grace. It is a moment of great freedom. It is a moment made for open arms and wild-eyed explorers of a cosmos filled with red nebulae and black holes.

Conversion is the opening of the heart to the grace of new possibilities. It does not blame God for plotting nefarious plans to test and try and torment us. It recognizes in the glory of new life that God simply companions us, simply stands by ready to receive our tattered, restless selves, as we are tested, tried, and tormented by the machinations of life itself. God guides us to new life by allowing us to open our eyes to possibility and find it for ourselves.

The important thing to understand is that conversion is not always immediate. It can even be impossible, sometimes for years. But the longer we put it off, the longer we resist change, the longer it takes for us to become more than we were when the struggle began.

Change is an invitation to see life differently now than I did before. It stretches my vision and opens my heart to what I could not see in life before life picked me up and put me down in the middle of it: I go to Africa and begin to see black people differently. I work with a Muslim and begin to see Islam differently. I lose what I have clung to for my security for years and begin to see myself differently. Change converts me from the narrowness of perspective that trapped me in the small confines of my former self to a more expansive, more flexible citizen of the world. It calls me to imagination.

And so when conversion comes, I finally discover that there is more than one way to be in the world. I learn, perhaps with some chagrin, that there is more than "the American way," more than "a man's way," more than "my way" of doing things. I open my arms to the rest of the world and it reaches down and takes me in.

The implications of such a spirituality of struggle are profound. For example: When the United States is attacked we ask ourselves how we might be in the world in such a way that frustration of this magnitude would never rise again. We ask what we are not seeing that would make religious fanaticism seductive to the poor and oppressed. Similarly, when my own life comes to a dead end, I ask myself how much I am willing to learn in order to begin again. When the world as I have known it, inside or out, spins and tilts, I ask myself what there is in the new one for me to trust and try. Peter Medawar reminds us that "Today the world changes so quickly that in growing up we take leave not just of youth but of the world we were young in. . . . Fear and resentment of what is new is really a lament for the memories of our childhood."[1] It's a sobering thought. Change, struggle, conversion have become the spiritual hinges of the new century on which hang not just our present but our past as well.

Change is of the essence of life. Or as Herbert Spencer put it in his *Principles of Biology:* "A living thing is distinguished from a dead thing by the multiplicity of the changes at any moment taking place in it."[2] A commitment to changelessness is not only unfortunate, it is impossible. Rigidity is its sin; death is its wages.

We cannot not change. But we can refuse to be converted. We can allow ourselves to become dogmatic. We can refuse to make Jacob's journey to a new land, having been evicted from an old one. We can become the spiritual corpses of a creative God who goes on endlessly creating, in us as well as around us.

It isn't that conversion is immediate. It is simply that the spiritual person is open to the possibility. I admit that I have gone back often in my mind to the crossroads created by that determining phone call. I have looked back at that other possibility — to life as a writer of fiction — and wondered if, in the end, the first road of characters and stories, of plots and themes, would not have been more meaningful, more beautiful, more effective. I have no way at all of knowing that. All I know is that essays are lovely things and I have learned a great deal by writing them. I have become more open, more knowledgeable, more

1. Sir Peter Medawar, *Pluto's Republic* (1982).
2. Herbert Spencer, *Principles of Biology* (1865).

thoughtful, more aware of the God who stands by. I have learned that there is more than one way to do a thing. "Wisdom," Octavio Paz said, "lies neither in fixity nor in change, but in the dialectic between the two."[3]

3. Octavio Paz, *Times,* London, 8 June 1989.

6. The Struggle of Isolation

S truggle is a very private thing. It happens in the very depths of our souls. It comes with the loss of what we have thought to be of such significance that we cannot abide the thought of life without it. Other people commiserate, of course, as they watch us struggle with the pain of losing, the meaning of endings, the shock of great change, the emptiness of the present. But they cannot really share our pain because what we have lost, however significant to us is not really significant to them. What we lose is ours and ours alone: our dream, our hope, our expectation, our property, our identity. All private. All personal. All uniquely and singularly ours. Our friends look on caringly, of course, but there's little else they can do. They advise but they cannot possibly know the cost of every step. It is not their arms that are heavy, not their legs that have gone to lead, not their "knees that are weak" (Psalm 109).

They talk to us about going on but they do not understand that the thought of going on is unimportant to us now. If anything, it is what we least want to do; indeed, it seems impossible. And, as far as we are concerned, it is certainly not desirable anymore. Go on for what reason? Those others who stand at the edges of our life at such a time as this cannot realize the sense of deep, deep isolation that comes when life as we have known it has been suddenly extinguished.

There is no one who can take the pain away because the pain cannot be taken away. There is no one there to ease it because it simply cannot be eased.

Desperate to help, they tell us how insignificant the thing was that we staked our lives upon. "It doesn't matter," they say. "You'll have another one." As in child or house or job or lover or dream. "It isn't worth it," they tell us. Or, at their best, they remind us that "time will heal the pain," and how we "will learn to live with" the loss. But, oh, how wrong they are! I gave my life to it. Surely my life was worth something. "This is unjust," they agree, but injustice happens nevertheless. No one changes it. No one confronts it. No one does a thing but commiserate. And that only for a while. In the end, we are alone. Just I and the struggle. Just I and the violence, the emptiness, the rage within me. "And Jacob was left alone," the biblical story tells us. Indeed.

I worked with a woman who had been a victim of incest in her early grade school years. An older brother, home from the seminary, began to molest her when she was eight years old. Old enough to have the beginnings of a conscience, not old enough to know sin from act. He was the apple of his Catholic mother's eye. So no help there. He was the paragon of family virtue but he was doing to her what she had been told was mortal to her soul. And so, time after time she feared more for her eternal salvation than she did for her present preservation. She would gladly have died to stop the sin but she could not tell a mother who, she was sure, would have blamed her for lying about him, not him for abusing her. This woman was seventy years old before she told me about it and sobbed in my office while she did. All her life, she said, she had been afraid that everyone who passed her in the hall could see what she had done. She had been doing angry penance all her life for something that was not her fault. All her life she had lived in isolation, wrestling with the writhing in her soul. All her life she had been in pain. All her life she had been alone in her agony.

I put my arms around her while she sobbed but I never thought for a moment that there was any way in the world that I could take away those years of lonely despair. We went on talking about it, of course. We worked for a sense of wholeness, a new perspective on the self, a feeling of internal, personal goodness. And the ongoing conversations, the support, the acceptance seemed to give her little bursts of well-being. But down deep, the wounds never really healed; the scars never went away.

Scientists have known for decades the effects of isolation, both physical and emotional. Infants denied physical contact die. People deprived of emotional support stand to slip into a reality of their own. They withdraw from the social circle whose plastic smiles and good times and uncare they cannot abide. They begin to resent laughter, as wounded by others' enjoyment as they are by the sufferings with which they are still dealing. After all, who has a right to laugh in the face of such hurt? They begin to trade in fantasy. They slip in and out of the memories that haunt them. One day they are gentle and communicative. The next day they are hostile and sour. Alone with what they cannot put down, they relive it and its shock and its wounds day after day after day.

Isolation is not simply a physical event that cuts us off from sensory stimulation. Isolation also shrinks the psyche itself. It cages us round with bitterness. Cut off from the rest of the human race, we stand frozen in our tracks, left to mourn what was while the rest of the world goes on without us, oblivious, helpless, and as far as we can tell, uncaring. Some never sense the pain in us at all. Some see the hurt but have no balm to bring to it. Some diminish it or despise it or ignore it. It doesn't quite matter which — the effects are all the same. In the end, struggle is private.

But struggle is also public. When the foundations of our world begin to shake — when relationships end, when long-held beliefs no longer satisfy, when our securities vanish — our ability to deal with the remainder of our world begins to shudder, too. Life-management crises in one area have a way of seeping over into other areas like a drop of ink in a gallon of water. One struggle colors everything.

Reality becomes blurred. We live in our losses, our pain, our memories, our lost hopes. We run or we lean. Most of all, like children burned on a stove or animals subjected to shock collars, we take no chances now on anything that might hurt us the same way again. We shun love, fear organizations, stop our work, burn our plans, avoid the very things we love most, keep our distance from whatever might tempt us to try again, to begin over, to trust.

But if isolation becomes one kind of refuge, dependence is another. Either we close people out of our lives or we become totally compliant, totally apathetic. We shut ourselves off from the rest of the world or we give ourselves over entirely to its excesses. Judgment fails us; social paralysis sets in. The drinking starts, the smoking begins, the all-night movies drown out the need for sleep and the memories that haunt us, the pain that taunts us in the darkness. We become disoriented and begin to call friends for directions about the smallest things in life: How to write a check, how to read a recipe, how to get the furnace fixed, what to have for dinner. Having lost one dimension of life, we allow people to direct us through the rest of it and so we give whatever little remains of our once-confident lives away. Where is the way out of this morass? Where is the end of the pain? Where is life when all of life has been destroyed?

The spiritual response is too often a simplistic one: either we abandon God or we blame God for abandoning us. "I beg you, tell me your name," Jacob pleads with the spirit with which he wrestles. But he gets no answer. Nor do we. We find no cause to cure us, no one to accuse, no way to respond. And, alone with ourselves, we like ourselves less and less every day.

I walked the banks of the creek that ran through the camp morning after morning that summer, fighting waves of depression, angry about where I was, and totally uninterested in anything going on around me. Just one thing was sure: I would not be cooking. I had never cooked even an egg in my life. "Third cook" meant scrubbing floors and doing the pots and pans. The world went to dead in me. There was nothing here that gave me joy, nothing I wanted to do, nothing that could ease either the pain of the loss or the fear of a future that meant simply more of the same.

Every morning I prayed a psalm out loud to myself as the stream gushed by, never more aware of the feelings of the psalmist in my life. "I was up to my neck in seaweed," I read in Psalm 69, "and you saved me." I wanted to believe that I would be saved but just then, I could not. After all, there was no way of bringing back the hopes of a lifetime, no way of retrieving what had been taken unceremoniously away. I could leave religious life, of course, but that would be to give up the rest of what was a very satisfying life for having lost a part of it. It was dilemma beyond dilemma.

Such junctures are dangerous times, both psychologically and spiritually. We are in the grips of a strange force to which we would be just as happy to surrender. We are caught in the vortex of an inner storm. Having lost the dream, we risk losing the balance of ourselves, as well. We stand on the brink of losing the future as well as the past. And that is the temptation of struggle.

We find ourselves alone in a fragile world not of our own making, an unfriendly place where the sun no longer shines for us. What can possibly be the gift of such a state? It is the call out of isolation into independence. It is the grace of discovering that our lives are more than any one event and that we, not fate, are really what will determine what the rest of our lives will be like.

7. The Gift of Independence

⤺

Vonetta Flowers, a young African-American track star from Alabama, failed to qualify for the Sydney 2000 Summer Olympics. It was a devastating time for her; years of preparation were lost in a matter of seconds. The simple disappointment of missing the games, never mind the medals, was enough to break her heart and plunge her into depression. But instead of despairing, in that year's Winter Olympics she tried out for the bobsled team. It was a sport she had never even seen, let alone attempted. Yet Flowers became the first black American to win a gold medal for bobsledding in the Winter Olympics.

Did she achieve her heart's desire or not?

John Walsh, father of a young son kidnapped off his own street in a small rural community, channeled his sorrow and his rage into launching the first national organization for missing children. The government had never done it. Law enforcement agencies had not done it. But Walsh did it and because of him countless children have been returned safely to their homes.

Was his struggle worth it or not?

Lisa Beamer, mother of two small children and six months pregnant with the third, was widowed in the terrorist attacks in September 2001. Her husband, Todd, led the effort to down the third of the attack planes over Pittsburgh before it could be used to bomb another government building. Several months after his death and before the birth of their third baby, Lisa Beamer began a charitable foundation in his name, the purpose of which is to help other families who find themselves left to cope with disaster with limited resources and heavy hearts.

Was isolation her response to struggle?

Struggle faces us with choices. Hard choices. "There can be no growth without resistance," the Chinese proverb teaches us. The thought compels. Struggle is a fact of life. What we struggle against, what we struggle for, what we struggle with, all test and hone us. It is the resistance itself that seasons us. The great choice with which struggle confronts us, then, is not whether to accept it — struggle comes unbidden. It doesn't matter whether we accept it. The choice is whether to crumble under it or to brave it.

Struggle is an unsparing lesson but a necessary gift. It is not a gift which at first sight we want. With the coming of the Human Potential Movement in the 1960s, rigid self-discipline gave way to unrestrained emotional expression. The social norm of cerebral self-control and privacy found itself challenged by a new ethic of full disclosure. It was one excess following another. Having learned to be controlled to the extreme in the name of mental health and spiritual virtue, we were now being encouraged to be just as extreme in our display of emotions.

Strangers came together in weekly workshops to reveal to one another their most secret fantasies, their most shameful actions. They shouted one another down, gave way to inner angers a lifetime in coming, "let it all hang out." Satisfying the emotional demands of the moment, the gurus of the movement told us, is the measure of our humanity. It did not work.

Too often, people withdrew from the encounters more hurt, more rejected, more emotionally confused than ever. Now they knew intimacy but not love. Worse, now they were left with old wounds newly opened and not a clue about what to do with them in the future.

They had expressed their emotions but they had not struggled with them. They had revealed their hurts but they had not worked through them. They had exposed their agonies but had not put them down. They had lost control of themselves and gained nothing to put in its place. Feelings oozed out of people like oil, over everyone and everything they touched, but the pain remained and the soul stayed dry. There was clearly something missing. The expression of feelings was simply not enough to dispel the suffering.

The notion that to suppress feelings is to distort human development ignored an entire stream of spiritual literature on holy indifference. The ancient Christian virtue of detachment became at least suspect, often anathema.

From Clement of Alexandria in the second century, to Meister Eckhart in the thirteenth, to Ignatius of Loyola in the sixteenth, the idea of spiritual indifference — openness to the many manifestations of the will of God in life — has been a respected one. There were many ways to the end, not simply one, the spiritual theory taught, all of them good, some of them better than others from one moment to the next. The marrow of the spiritual life was to determine which of life's many possibilities were most suitable to the will of God in the present situation. The root of the exercise was "holy indifference," awareness of the multiple gifts of God and openness to all of them.

This is a spirituality with enduring psychological value as well.

The isolation that marks any serious struggle is a call to recognize that life is full of gifts that come and go, come and go as we ourselves come and go through the many stages of life. Detachment from the idea that there is only one way for me to go through life joyfully is its key. The pain of loss is a real and a present thing. It manacles my soul and breaks my heart, yes. But holy indifference — detachment — teaches me that there is no room for isolation, abandonment, death of the spirit when I lose one thing because I know that there is something else waiting for me in its place. If only I can allow myself to watch for it, to wait for it, to grasp it when it comes.

Designed to enable a person to regard all of life with an open mind and a willing heart, detachment — holy indifference — is the foundation of spiritual discernment. To discern is to choose between available options on the grounds that both are good but that one is more likely at this time to be preferable. It is the willingness to accept the idea that one option is more likely to result in greater growth at this particular time than can be expected from the other under these prevailing conditions, though both are good possibilities. Discernment and detachment are lifelines out of the pit of loss and the island of isolation to which it threatens to doom us.

Detachment teaches us to let go. Let go of unwavering answers. Let go of present achievements. Let go of life's little hoards of trinkets.

Let go of the now which is frozen in emotion for the sake of a future freed from old chains. It is the ability to see that there are many things of value in our lives, some of them more suited to one time than to another.

Discernment is based on the awareness that we cannot always have what we want, true, but also that there is enduring, sometimes hidden, always surprising spiritual value in what we do have. Discernment asks us to love many things for many different reasons and to choose what is the best of them for this instance.

The important mark of discernment is that it involves choice. It involves independence of judgment, the ability to maintain breadth of vision even in the midst of crisis, the awareness that we are not enslaved to our past. We can dream again. We can go on without leaning, without withering. We can summon up from within ourselves parts of ourselves that have yet to see the light of life. It means that despite the depth of our struggles, we must come out of our insulating isolation and live again or we shall have died, no matter how long we live.

Isolation erodes spiritual independence. In fact, it is dependence of the highest, most destructive order. Isolation blocks us from moving in the present because we are dependent on the past, trapped in the past. Or, it means that having fallen into isolation, we do not move newly into the present because we have chosen instead to be dependent on the world around us. We have chosen to be carried rather than to stand. We have chosen to give up on ourselves, to let other people carry us rather than to take care of ourselves. We deny or overlook or ignore the gift of independence, the place of detachment, in human development.

Isolation leaves us feeling cut off from the human race, aloof, withdrawn, at the mercy of the universe. Independence, on the other hand, emerges out of an awareness that there are other things to live for and we have within ourselves the ability to reach out and grasp them, if only we will.

Over the centuries, detachment lost its spiritual glow. Distorted by the excesses of extreme asceticism but at the same time, paradoxically, always regarded in its classical sense not as a way to deny the world but as the spiritual key to living in it more freely, detachment became the counterfeit coin of the happy life. It dampened feelings rather than sharpened them, its critics said — and not without reason. Jansenism, with its emphasis on ascetic discipline, became popular among French Catholics in the eighteenth century. In the name of holiness, it suppressed emotions rather than listened to them. It rendered the world dour and living an act of denial. In doing so it destroyed what is needed most in a time of struggle: the will to live because the world is bountiful. Detachment based on negation rather than an awareness of endless abundance is not a solution. At its healthiest, the human spirit is irrepressible and the human heart seeks hope, not desolation, however disguised dearth may be in the trappings of holiness.

But the truth remains: Nothing lasts. No single thing can consume our entire life's meaning. No single thing can give us total satisfaction. Nothing is worth everything: neither past, nor present nor future. It isn't true that the loss of any single thing will destroy us. Everything in life has some value and life is full of valuable things, things worth living for, things worth doing, things worth becoming, things worth loving again. It is only a matter of being detached enough from one thing to be open to everything else.

The essence of life is not to find the one thing that satisfies us but to realize that nothing can ever completely satisfy us. And that's all right.

No, I don't write fiction anymore but I have written a great number of other things, and I have loved every minute of it.

8. The Struggle of Darkness

⌘

The great interruptions of life leave us completely disoriented. We become lost. The map of life changes overnight and our sense of direction and purpose goes with it. Life comes to a halt, takes on a new and indiscernible shape. Promise fails us and it is the loss of promise that dries in our throats. What was is no more and what is to come, if anything, is unclear. All the things we depended on to keep us safe, to show us the way, to give us a reason for going on, disappear. If the baby dies, I have no idea why I am still alive either. If the relationship ends, I am ashamed of my undesirability and hide my face from the rest of the world. If the job I love ends, I have no idea what to do with my life from one day to the next. If the promotion fails to materialize, I can no longer understand where I am really going — or whether I am going anywhere at all. If the government tells me that the nation is at war and the markets have failed and left me penniless in my old age, I understand only two things in my helpless rage: that there must be enemies somewhere and that they have managed to destroy me though see them I can't and know them I don't. If the country is attacked, I know I am not safe but I don't know why or how. If illness downs me before my time, I drown in the helplessness of it. If the knock of death comes at the door, I am left plunged in black loneliness, the life behind me a little thinner now, the life before me a little less welcoming. Through it all, I find myself blindfolded and spinning somewhere in an inner space I have never known before. Like Jacob, I find myself in darkness. There is no God here.

We find ourselves on a wet, grey slope of sliding clay, being towed under, being swallowed up and taken down, no towline to save us. Who has not known this helpless, sinking feeling? Who has not known the God of Absence? Who has not felt abandoned by God?

The struggle now is to negotiate darkness of spirit. The ancients called it the dark night of the soul, this process of shedding everything in life but God. It is the moment of personal crucifixion in which we finally say out loud what we most fear: that there is no God, at least not here, not now. "My God, my God, why have you forsaken me?" becomes a personal cry. In the depths of pain, we suddenly find that this universe is, at base, a gross and teasing thing, purposeless, unguided, unwanted, uncared for. We doubt the God of losses. We doubt the notion of any God at all. We certainly doubt that God has anything real to do with us. If there is a God, it is a God who laughs at butterflies impaled on a board.

Sitting on the banks of the creek, psalms in hand, the summer of my appointment to camp rather than to the university, I struggled long and hard between the value of what I wanted and the value of what I had. God had become a question mark, not a certainty. Religious life had become cruel, not fulfilling. As I tried to pray, shaken, isolated, and in darkness, I could feel the dust of my soul under my tongue. I crawled into bed numb, the sun still high, every night. There was no reason to stay up. The next morning I had all I could do simply to get out of bed. There was no reason to begin another day. I could run away, of course, or I could stay. But I hardly had the energy for either. And neither response seemed to be a solution to anything. I simply went on breathing. My body went on living but my soul had died in a darkness so thick I could not see through it.

But the mystics also taught that this dark night was a necessary moment in the development of the soul. Sure of the absence of God, we actually become aware of the presence of God. It is the paradox of faith. It is the fortunate misadventure of life. By losing everything, we come to the realization that everything is far less than we think it is and far more than we ever dreamed it could be. In the end, everything is what cannot be taken away, what cannot be lost, what will not fail us in our hope. Everything is the nagging awareness that always there is more and that I already have it. I am reduced by misery to stop and look through the darkness to the light on the horizon that never changes. Darkness becomes the incubator of light.

Darkness is the winter of the soul, the time when it seems that nothing is growing. But winter, we know, is the fallow time of year. Winter is the time when the earth renews itself. And so it is with struggle. Unbeknownst to us, struggle is the call and the signal that we are about to renew ourselves. Whether we want to or not.

In wintertime, the horizon is at its starkest. It holds nothing of promise. All that can be seen are bare trees, grey rock, stripped soil. And yet somehow, it is the beckoning edge of the world. It is precisely the direction toward which we must move if we are ever to transcend the sterility of the view, the bouldery of the climb. Winter is a lesson about the fine art of loss and growth. Its lesson is clear: There is only one way out of struggle and that is by going into its darkness waiting for the light and being open to new growth.

Struggle is what forces us to attend to the greater things in life, to begin again when life is at its barest for us, to take the seeds of the past and give them new growth. And people do. I met a young woman from a wealthy family who, having been abandoned for adoption by a woman too poor to keep her, gave up her inheritance money to subsidize social justice projects. A couple whose own childhoods had been bereft of love and stability refused career promotions in favor of positions that allowed them both to have equal time with their children. A retired general who had seen the fruitless horrors of war spent the rest of his life in the peace movement.

We fear darkness and we avoid it. Nothing chills the soul more than lightlessness. It threatens our confidence. It jeopardizes our sense of self-sufficiency. To be in new space, to be where we do not know the contours of the place, cannot see the exit sign, cannot control the environment shakes us to our roots. We become pawns in the hands of the great unknown. And then, just then, we begin to believe in God in a whole new way. Darkness is the call to faith.

9. The Gift of Faith

Folklore teaches with great confidence that crises plunge us into faith. But the notion that there are no atheists in foxholes has all the comfort of a cliché and like most clichés offers little data to confirm the hope. Godfrey Diekmann, a legendary Benedictine liturgist, recounted being sunk up to his hips in a swamp while gathering watercress and having to be pulled out by a truck hoist. It was delicate and dangerous business. In the Christmas letter he wrote following the event he said that after more than fifty years of monastic life, "What bothers me is that during the entire ordeal of about twenty-five minutes I didn't have a single pious thought!"[1] Funny, perhaps, but commonly true. And not necessarily a bad thing at all. Even when we live in the presence of God our entire lives, there is no sudden spiritual awareness when the hard times come. There is just more of the same.

The truth is that it is not so much that darkness demands a faith response from us that matters. It is the kind of faith we demonstrate under pressure that counts. I saw a kind of faith once that defied all the psychology I'd ever been taught, all the theological definitions I'd ever learned. It seeped into my own faith-life like mist, illuminated the dark places, and clung to my soul like ether.

She was writhing on the floor in her bedroom by the time I got

---

1. Patrick Henry, *The Ironic Christian's Companion: Finding the Marks of God's Grace in the World* (1999).

there. Her elbows were tight against her ribs, her fists were clenched, she was rolling back and forth, from side to side, and moaning. She was a gentle woman, a kind of Dresden doll. She'd been a first grade teacher all her life. She had reared generation after generation just by the lilt of her smile. Years later they were still coming back to adore her. But she was also manic-depressive. She had been in and out of hospitals all her life, on one medication after another for years. When drugs became available the periods between the laughter and the deep, deep gloom became longer. But never permanent. Over the years, as she got older, the chemical balance became harder and harder to maintain. Then she would become depressed to the point of heartbreak. The doctors would admit her to the hospital, withdraw her from her current medicine, and, only when she was completely purged of a previous drug, start again to find the right dosage for the new prescription. It took a long time to do. They were frightening and painful periods for her. The pain, the gloom, the despair, the depression, the writhing, all became part of the routine.

But for all the regularity of it, I had never seen her this bad before. I got down on my knees beside her and took her by the shoulders. "Come on, Theresie," I said. "Time to go to the doctor again." The wail came from the center of her. "No!" she insisted. "No! Don't make me do that. I can't do that. I hate that." I began to rock her a little. "Theresie," I crooned, "the doctor is worried about you. He wants you in the hospital." She stiffened. "I know he's worried," she sobbed. "He won't believe me. He thinks I want to commit suicide! I've tried to explain to him but he won't listen." She shuddered a deep breath. "Joan, tell him. Tell him! I would never do that. I have too much faith in God to do that!" I couldn't see her for the tears in my own eyes. She was a holy woman and I knew she was telling the truth. She really did have too much faith in God to do that. She knew she was not being punished, not being abandoned, not being tested, not being scourged. She knew she was sick and she knew that God was with her in the midst of the darkness of it.

The God who turns red lights green at our command is not the God Theresie worshipped. The God who gives points for good behavior is not the God she knew. Her God was the loving Creator in whose energy and life "we live and move and have our being" (Acts 17:28).

Her God did not manipulate life, but rather gave it and then enabled her to live it out, learning as she went, loving as she did. Her God was the creator of the seasons — the One because of whom winter always turned into spring.

This creative God is the One who made us co-creators of this created universe. We cooperate in the seeding of life. We participate in the coming of justice. We cultivate the ground. God created the world, yes, but then gave it to us to develop. We have made it what it is.

It is faith in this God that raises us from our tombs of oppression and sadness and want and fear and pain to begin again doing our part to make the world a laughing, loving place.

There is no reason to assume, for example, that God will end nuclear weaponry. If the world ends in a nuclear blast, it will not be this God who did it. We created nuclear weapons; we can end them ourselves. There is no reason to blame God for the inequality between women and men, blacks and whites, the rich and the poor. God made all of us out of the same human substance; it is we who have put one under the heel of the other on the specious grounds of natural inferiorities. In the light of everything we have been given, we have no grounds for blaming God for our losses. As W. H. Auden put it: "May it not be that, just as we have to have faith in God, God has to have faith in us and, considering the history of the human race so far, may it not be that 'faith' is even more difficult for God than it is for us?"[2]

The call to faith is not the call to surrender to a grinning, ghoulish God who tries creation for the sheer delight of trial. It is the call to believe, like Jacob who struggles through the night, that though we are in darkness, the dawn will come in its due time. For if God is in the depth of the heart, no amount of darkness can extinguish that presence. On the contrary, it may actually intensify our intuition of it. The sense of losing God may be exactly what draws us back to God, though we cannot imagine it at the time. "Why do you ask my name?" the stranger says to Jacob. The source of the struggle is not what is at issue. It is the value of struggling that grows us.

Never for a moment, sitting by the creek that ran through a children's camp, head down, heart heavy, did I think that God had

2. W. H. Auden, *A Certain World* (1970).

changed my life. I knew exactly who had changed my life. All I knew is that I had been born with something God-given. And the God who gave me that gift, I believed, would give me the insight to somehow bring it to life. Because I wanted it? No, because it could not be otherwise and still be me.

What are we called to believe and in whom? We are surely called to believe that God who is everywhere is with us. And we are called to believe that this God is Energy and Love. Not the Grand Inquisitor. Not the great Circus Master. Not the Indifferent Professor who does distant research on our lives. God is the One who made for us a good world and walks with us to hold us up as we go. Sometimes, in the face of the God of life, the most faithful thing we can do is simply to keep on living.

10. *The Struggle with Fear*

◆

Alone, in the dark, at the mercy of an unknown enemy, and engaged in a grueling contest, Jacob faces the fact that he is in the struggle of his life. There is no certainty that he will survive it, no real awareness of how best to proceed. Surrender is possible, of course, but to what purpose, at what cost to the future? This is home. This is his land. This is his responsibility. Flight is a possibility, but to where? Everything he cares about — his wives, his children, his servants, his herd — is here. We understand the situation only too well. We, too, know what it is like at times to have only one real option: to be forced to stay in the struggle and see this thing through, however formidable the situation, however frightening the prospects. There may be no life to be had here, but there is no promise of life anywhere else, either. There is nothing to do but to keep on going through the notions, knowing that at any minute we may collapse on the dustheaps of the world we ourselves have made.

Who hasn't had the feeling? Fear paralyzes a person. It is confrontation with the great unknown and it can be devastating. If I say what's bothering me where and when it ought to be said, what will happen to me? If I give my honest opinion in the group, will they ever invite me back? If I dare to say no, will the marriage ever be the same again? If I don't parrot the party line — any party line, political, corporate, ecclesiastical — will I ever again have a place in the system, a seat at the table, a life of honor and appreciation? What am I willing to lose in order to have peace of mind, integrity of soul? These are hard questions, all of them, and none of them without substance. They are the questions that test the fiber of the soul.

It's not the grappling with a thing that defeats us; it is the unknown answers to the hidden questions that wear us down. When people are willing to engage with a question, when there are voices in the chorus behind our own, when our concerns are taken seriously, then any amount of effort is not too much to ask. But when, like the wrestler who grapples with Jacob, there is no will to stay in the discussion to the end, to work it through, to figure it out, then fear for the sake of the question, for the sense of the self, beckons.

I understand the situation only too well. For years now I have had a recurring nightmare. Every time I am at the top of some variety of freestanding staircase or ladder or fire escape. It is swaying precariously back and forth. I am alone and frightened and I want down. But, I realize, there are missing rungs beneath me and the precipice is sheer. I am sick from the swaying and afraid of the height. Other people in the dream, I know, have managed either to go on beyond this place to the next level or to descend to levels of stability and safety. But I cling, frozen in open space, to the top while the staircase groans and pitches under my feet and my knees go to water. There the dream drifts away, over and over and over again. But even when I'm finally lucky enough to wake, it lingers within me.

I am convinced that the ladder is a metaphor for what it means to find ourselves grappling with the great struggles of life, exposed to the storm and incapable of ignoring it. It is the intuition that the world is shifting and changing under my feet, and that I am in both personal and public danger because of it. It is the sense of rootless swaying and unconscious consciousness that every next step chances hollow ground. And it is at the same time the price to be paid for the foolish, stubborn, delirious desire to stand still there regardless. It is what we do when there is nothing else that can possibly be done. His soulfulness in combat with fear.

Fear cripples us more than any disease ever could. It takes eminent good sense and turns it to gelatin. Or it takes utter sincerity and turns it into simpering sycophancy. Fear tempts us to sell our souls in exchange for the grossly lesser prize of false security. We see it as security because it buys us time. But it is false because those who refuse to honor our questions will refuse to honor our person any time it suits their needs. Worse, fear keeps us from being who we ourselves really want to be. Fear keeps us from being someone we ourselves can admire. Fear is the contest between good sense, as in "Don't do anything foolish," and a good heart, as in "Don't do anything small." Sense we can live without, greatness we cannot.

We struggle with fear of criticism as we try to hide our inadequacies, even from ourselves. We struggle with the fear of ridicule remembered from grade school playgrounds and transferred from there to the playgrounds of life. We struggle with the fear of being different — the one woman in a group of men, for instance — in a culture that sells sameness on every billboard in the nation. We struggle with the fear of authority in a period where authority, having become technologically pervasive, has gone rampant and intrudes on every fine point of life.

But we stay at the dizzying heights of our souls, clinging to the swaying ladders of our worlds because we know that something has gone vastly wrong. We know that we have already given over too much of ourselves to an authority beneath the real authority of our souls.

Oppressors do not get to be oppressors in a single sweep. They manage it because little by little, we make them that. We overlook too much in the beginning and wonder why we lose control in the end.

On the public level, these dim, distant "authorities" threaten our very world. We are faced now, for instance, with the potential for cataclysmic destruction from the nuclear weapons of "rogue" nations — poor and desperate countries for whom death is fast becoming more desirable than life — because, having profited from them ourselves, we refused to confront them. Now they are the backbone of the worldwide modern military arsenal and we are held hostage to our own designs.

On a personal level, authorities free of accountability bind our souls. They keep us in servitude to a bogus notion of superiority. They claim a power to which they have no right and engage us in the collusion. Our fear of them is a measure of our own moral maturity, or our lack of it. But moral maturity requires us to choose truth over self-preservation, whatever the cost. It faces us with the responsibility to choose new heights of conscience over personal comfort.

When I was a young woman, I was afraid. I didn't even ask why the university matriculation had been denied me. Instead I slunk quietly away to do listlessly what I did not want to do at all. By doing nothing constructive, nothing honest, I doomed myself to depression, yes, but on a larger scale I made authority omnipotent. I forsook the responsibility to honor my own inner authority. And I almost lost the struggle for conscience.

But as the years went by, I knew I had made a mistake. I began to understand the damage that the sin of silence inflicts. I had lived through the Hitler regime and its end in the Holocaust that the Western world had long refused to acknowledge. As a student of church history, I knew what had happened because, afraid for their own lives, whole societies ignored the Inquisition, the Crusades, witch burnings, slavery, and segregation. As a student of world history, I knew what had happened because, stripped of a sense of personal accountability, officials and citizens, advisors and experts, voters and small-town politicians, preferred "following orders" to challenging Hitler's "Final Solution," to leaking the Bay of Tonkin lie, to exposing Watergate, to refusing to press nuclear buttons. From these examples I learned that fear of authority was not a good enough reason for anything. I came to understand that I would have to speak the truth as I saw it every small moment along the way.

Clearly there is a gift that beckons in the struggle with fear. It is courage. Or, as Friedrich Dürrenmatt wrote, "This is the only art we have to master nowadays: to look at things without fear and to fearlessly do right."[1] It is the call to courage that is the seedbed of hope.

---

1. Friedrich Dürrenmatt, *Romulus the Great* (1964).

11. *The Gift of Courage*

⁓

We collect stories of courage like treasures from the deep. We guard them as part of the collective memory that makes all of us more human. I carry in my heart an image of a young man standing in front of a tank in Tiananman Square in Beijing. I think of him and breathe a purer air. I see in my mind's eye a clear-headed John Dean standing before a Senate commission on campaign violations and giving testimony that would not only lead to the downfall of a presidency but end his own political career as well. I stand with the women at Greenham Common in the rain. They have already been there outside the military base for over a year protesting the nuclearization of England. I am there only for the day. I remember young black men, all in white shirts and ties, being beaten for sitting at a lunch counter in segregated Alabama.

Of course, I see them as I sit in my living room watching TV. I have lit the eternal flame in Yad Vashem but only as a part of a delegation long safe from such barbarity. I have walked through the Garden of the Righteous in Jerusalem, the memorial of trees planted in memory of those Gentiles who saved Jews from the Holocaust, but only as a tourist. I have been through the Palestinian refugee camps on the West Bank and seen brave people live with great dignity in total squalor. True, I have seen courage on a grand scale. But I have seen it in far smaller but no less significant ways, as well — all of it born in struggle, all of it enkindled by fear. It is when we are most

49

afraid of something that we know that only courage is the correct response.

Courage is the capacity to stand our ground, to speak the truth, even in the face of overwhelming odds. It is the sight of Jacob holding fast to the stranger with whom he struggles demanding information that the stranger will not give. "Tell me your name," Jacob demands over and over again, to no avail. It is, in other words, the intention to stay at a thing, like a tick buried in fur, whatever the cost — until death, if necessary. It is in the staying itself that we also discover what it is to wrest the self, the problem, this pain, from the refuge of darkness. Then, we discover what it is to wrestle it to the ground within ourselves until, stripped of all its masks, it can finally be resolved. Then, because we have refused to ignore it, refused to give it sway, all the tomorrows of the world will be better than its yesterdays, for the world in general, perhaps, or at least for our own small part of it.

Courage is not nearly so rare a quality as we sometimes like to think it is. We forgive ourselves the responsibility to muster it on the grounds that it is the unwonted virtue of unusual people in momentous circumstances. The truth is that courage is what carries simple people through an average day. It is not an action; it is an attitude. It is the spiritual strength that gives direction in the midst of confusion. It is no more uncommon than fear. It is, in fact, the child of fear.

Courage is a universal commodity. Children muster courage in the backyards of the world as they resist neighborhood bullies or face down rejection or survive the curse of being different. Old people bring courage to bear as they muster the audacity it takes to deal with ageism and ill health. Young people test their courage against social norms or corporate business practices. Each of us, every day, in one way or another, is called to courage. Courage is not an exceptional virtue. It is what makes the difference between a gracious and a noxious world. It drives us to reevaluate all the unchallenged assumptions of life, to confute the unacceptable, to confront the oppressive, and, if we do, eventually to change the unchangeable.

Courage is the counterpart of honesty. It counts character more important than acceptance. It speaks up when silence is the key to social approval. It is one word of disputation said about the effects of the national budget on national services at a cocktail party. It is one word in favor of women's rights at the local church dinner. It is one glimmer of doubt about the effects of globalization or the protection of civil rights in a democracy or a show of concern for welfare for the poor that we call food stamps as well as for the welfare for the rich that we call tax breaks.

Courage does not come in a burst of insight. Courage comes out of the way we think and the way we live from Sunday to Sunday, every week of our lives. I watched in horror, and in awe, as Mary Lou, one of my best friends, a veteran of the Vietnam War peace movement and a long-time proponent of nonviolent conflict resolution, slammed on the brakes in the middle of town, jumped out of the car, and moved quietly but quickly into the midst of a knife-swinging fight between two of the loudest and most belligerent of the town drunks. She stood between the two of them, talking peace to each of them, calmly and kindly, and they heard her. They walked away sulking but unhurt. And alive. She was shaking when she got back into the car, but smiling. Courage is what you do when your heart is ready.

Courage also implies our willingness to be honest with ourselves as well as with others. It requires that we learn to accept our limitations and to live within our boundaries. We are not everything we would like to be. We are not who we would like to be. Like the fine musician Salieri who exhausted and abased himself out of envy for the genius of the composer Mozart, we too often fail to develop, to enjoy, the talents we do have because we so much want to be something else. It takes a great deal of courage not only to stand against the odds with others but to accept the odds against ourselves.

Courage is not the lost part of ourselves; it is the hidden part of ourselves that only fear can energize. Fear is not the opposite of courage. Fear is the catalyst of courage.

We have all had our own small moments of courage, our icons of possibility. One experience in particular reminds me how easy it can really be to face my fears. Just by being honest enough to admit that I think differently about something, I take a first step into the heart of courage. Slated to give a public presentation in Texas one evening, I was being hosted in the hotel penthouse as part of the pre-banquet reception there. They were serving six-inch prawns on sterling silver platters, and tall canisters of champagne were going around like ice water. Men in silk shirts surrounded me, talking to one another over my head about the price of oil.

Suddenly Ronald Reagan appeared on the large television screens in the four corners of the room to announce that he had given the order that day that anyone attempting to cross the Rio Grande River into the United States would be shot on sight. "Well, it's about time that got stopped," one man said. "They come up here and take American jobs. Someone has to put an end to that," another said. "We've been warning them," a third said. "What else can we do but shoot them?" he pronounced confidently. I took a deep breath: "We could give Texas back," I said. Men turned and looked at me in total disbelief, in profound disagreement. There was a long, awkward silence. I held my breath. It was not polite talk in the present political arena, I knew. But down deep, inside, where it counts, I also knew that given the same conversation in the same place with the same people, I would say it all over again.

For years I had been taught that silence in the face of opposition is virtue. But I had failed my truest self once. I had stood silently by, a cardboard cutout of a person, as decisions were made around me and about me with never a word to me about my own best insights into the situation, my own awareness of what was best for the students I taught, my own clear notions of who I really was and how I might best fit into the world. In the interest of obedience and nicety and approval, I had not said a single word. I knew I would not betray my best self a second time.

Courage is coming to realize that what does and does not happen in the world does so because of what you and I fail to say — not when silence is right, but when we fear the cost to ourselves of speaking out.

12. *The Struggle with Powerlessness*

I stood on the small patch of grass in front of the little stone cottage and watched the fire run raging up the Irish mountainside behind it. The annual burn-off had gotten out of hand. The tiny little house with its great picture windows overlooking Derrynane Bay and its remnant of old mill lay almost surrounded by flames. They licked at the fringes of fuchsia on the front lawn. They raced through the gorse at the side of the house, circled the hill around us, flirted with the propane gas tank, and then jumped the road to the other side of the mountain below the Ring of Kerry. Johnny, the groundskeeper, and four local farmers scrambled up and down the face of the hill with small shovels. They beat at each burst of fire, one clump of grass at a time, trying in vain to save a bit of pastureland here, a fence there, a telephone pole along the rutted road. In front of us, the ocean swelled and mocked. All that water and no way to get a single drop of it where it was really needed. All we could do now was to wait for the fire to run its course. In a last-ditch effort to do something — to do anything — I called the owners in Dublin. "If there is anything special that you want me to take with me out of this house," I yelled into the phone, "tell me now. We may not have much time left to save it." The voice came back: "Glory be to God, just save yourself. Get out of there. Now."

Powerlessness is the grassfire of the soul. It brings us face to face with the frustration that comes when life is out of control. When the children seem to come unmoored from everything we think we've ever taught them, we lose a sense of our very selves. Who are we really, if we could not save them from this end, prevent them from becoming involved in these things? When we are well and strong one day and laid low the next with an illness because of which we will never be the same person again, we go grey in the heart. What kind of life do we have if we can't even manage the daily routine anymore? When the job goes and the money runs out, taking our social lives and our neighborhood with it, we crumble at our very centers. What will people think? How will we ever recover? When we lose the fight for justice with authorities who for all we can tell prefer power to people, we lose trust in any institution at all. What will stop the slide to the bottom after we have spent so much fierce energy getting to the top?

We have come, then, to the Jacob who wakes up in a struggle for his life, unaware of its coming, unprepared for its severity. Life as we knew it has gone to mist and there is nothing whatsoever that we can do about it. Nothing at all. It has all the promise of the strike of an iron club against a tree trunk. It resounds through the system with a great thudding uselessness. Nothing gives way. There is no out. There is no response at all — just the raw, dense awareness that for the first time in years, perhaps, we are again at the mercy of life itself.

The struggle with powerlessness is the struggle for effectiveness, yes, but more than that it is the struggle for simplicity of heart. However much we have cultivated an image of the imperious, the aura of invincibility, the patina of the supremely secure, we are helpless to help ourselves. Life as we have known it ends. We are confronted with the puniness of our existence. We come face to face with our mortality, our vulnerability, our limitations. Now we must become who we really are, not who we have presented ourselves to be. Now simplicity — our basic, core self — takes over.

But it is not an easy transition, this metamorphosis from the public self to the real self. We struggle against it all the way. We fear to expose our nakedness of soul, our lack of inner resources, our paucity of imagination. If, left on the dung heap of life, bereft of our trappings — our uniforms and titles and bank accounts and offices and resumes — we have no reason to go on living, then the question is whether we have ever lived at all. And that is the question that none of us ever want to ask.

Powerlessness strips away all pretenses and renders us human. And then it is indeed time to save ourselves. It is such a frightening place in which to find ourselves because it requires that we spend the rest of our lives making sure that underneath all the pomp and all the protocol of our public selves there is really something left to save. Otherwise we run the risk of never really coming to be a person at all until we have lost all the things that until this time have substituted for the self.

Powerlessness is such a burden to modern existence because it cleaves like a barnacle to the myth of control. Being in control, being independent, is a theme that runs through Western philosophy from the bowels of the Enlightenment to the brink of global chaos. It is a fantasy. The vision of being free of external restraints, of becoming breeders of a race of Atlases like Ayn Rand's, taints everything it touches. It turns individuals into narcissists and nations into economic parasites. We are a civilization that for centuries has used the resources of others for the sake of ourselves and then defended the right to do it in the name of national security. The Europeans took South American gold. The Japanese took the Russian fisheries. The Americans, calling it their Manifest Destiny, took vast amounts of land from the Native Americans and territory from Mexico. Having begun in feudal servitude, we have come to capitalistic arrogance. Whatever we saw, we wanted. Whatever we wanted, we took.

Finally, little by little, we all learned to do the same. The Robber Barons of the Industrial Revolution took lives one grueling day at a time for slave wages. Enron executives in the midst of the Technological Revolution sold off stock to engorge themselves with the pension money of the very workers who had made them rich. It is everyone for himself or herself now, it seems.

We see ourselves as figures in splendid isolation and we respond in horror when the powerless of the world, sick with their own frustration, topple our Trade Towers and turn our image of the world upside down. Then our fortresses fall and we know what we never knew before: we must do something before we are powerless to do a thing about the desperation of the powerless.

If we arc lucky, if the people whose lives we touch are lucky, we will suffer a taste of powerlessness in our own private lives. Because then things change. Then we begin to see with a gentler, broader vision and talk with a kinder tongue and feel with deeper feelings for those for whom powerlessness is a way of life. Then we look into ourselves and see what's there. And what isn't there, as well.

Powerlessness is a sickening feeling in the pit of the stomach. It is also a call to become something new. The gift of powerlessness invites us to enjoy the grace of surrender.

13. The Gift of Surrender

❧

One of the hardest moments in life, perhaps, is the one in which I discover that there are some things about which I can do nothing at all. There is no one, I come to realize with a kind of empty shock, on whom I can depend to do my bidding this time. Despite the network of people I have carefully constructed over the years, there is no one with connections enough to pull this final string for me. There is no one on earth, no matter how well-disposed they may be to me, who can make the inevitable go away. It is like losing at the Supreme Court of life. It is the closing of the last door. However much I protest, however wildly I resist, I cannot regain what I nevertheless refuse to lose. I simply go on, stuck in the fantasy I call my reality. If I decline to admit that things have changed, my tortured thinking suggests, perhaps they won't have. The least I can do is to punish the world for allowing the change by declining to accept it.

It took three years for Julia to take the baby, turn out the light, and move from the house after her long-gone young husband decided that he wasn't ready to be married and left them in it alone. Only, at long last, when she got a place of her own was life able to begin again. Part of the pain of any great struggle, in other words, is the reluctance to admit that we have been bested. Or at least that we have been bridled. The relationship is over. The divorce is final. The diagnosis is correct. The partner is dead. The money is gone. The friends have betrayed me. The job offer has been withdrawn. The house has been sold. The once great life-giving enterprise has ended. And there is nothing whatsoever that I can do about it. What I have now is all I have. And it is not what I want.

The spirit dies within me. I am convinced that I will never live again, no matter how long I go on breathing. What I do not know, ironically, is that this loss is more grace than I know, more grace than I can bear at the moment. It is this very loss that will open up a whole new world in me. Without it, there is no life to go on to at all. Only more of the barbed and suffocating same.

Surrender is what cleans off the barnacles that have been clinging to the soul. It is the final act of human openness. Without it I am doomed to live inside a stagnant world called the self. The problem is that the self is a product of my own making. I myself shape the self. I construct it one experience, one attitude, one effort at a time till the person I become — rich in reality or starved for it — is finished. I shape me, great or small, wizened or insulated, out of the tiny little measures of newness that I allow to penetrate the depths of my darknesses one dollop at a time. What I do not let into my world can never stretch my world, can never give it new color, can never fill it with a new kind of air, can never touch the parts of me that I never knew were there. What I once imagined must forever be, what I relived in memory for years, is no more. Openness saves me from the boundaries of the self and surrender to the moment is the essence of openness.

Surrender does not simply mean that I quit grieving what I do not have. It means that I surrender to new meanings and new circumstances, that I begin to think differently and to live somewhere that is totally elsewhere. I surrender to meanings I never cared to hear — or heard, maybe, but was not willing to understand. Try as I might to read more into someone's words than they ever really meant, I must surrender to the final truth: She did not love me. They do not want me. What I want is not possible. And, hardest to bear of all, all arguments to the contrary are useless. I surrender to the fact that what I lived for without thought of leaving, I have now lost. I surrender to the circumstances of life. Try as I might to turn back the clock, to relive a period of my life with old friends, in long-gone places, out of common memories, through old understandings and theologies and past ideals, I come to admit that such attempts are the myth of a mind in search of safer days. The way we were is over. The class is no longer a class. Communism is no longer a rallying cry. The good old days are only slivers of memory now. They are, in fact, now laughable to many, resented by some, essentially different in intimation to each of us.

Surrender is the crossover point of life. It distinguishes who I was from who I have become. Surrender comes in grand ways and in small ones but, sooner or later, I must admit that there is no turning back from the rejection or the loss or the turn of age or the abandonment. Life as I had fantasized it is ended. What is left is the spiritual obligation to accept reality so that the spiritual life can really happen in me.

Jacob wrestles all night long with no hope of really winning. At the end of the night, he is still in the struggle but ready finally to give it up without needing to triumph. He can just be what he is. It is enough, he understands, simply to persist rather than to need to overcome. To persist is to live in hope. To insist on overcoming the enemy, on the other hand, only dooms us to perpetual contention over something that may not have perpetual value. Not to us, not to anyone. I understand the situation. I surrendered, too: There would be no master's degree in creative writing. Not then. Probably never. But that did not mean that I was not a writer, simply that I was not then free to write one kind of writing. Surrender is the moment in which we realize that it is time to become someone new. Surrender is not about giving up; it is about moving on.

I learned surrender through a story that revolved around a far more final one than comes out of a change of plans or a shift in relationships or a loss of fortune. It was about the ultimate moving on which all the other surrendered dreams of life simply foreshadow. I remember the incident clearly to this day: I was a new prioress at the time. The days' appointments were still basically routine interviews. People came to talk about ministry changes or vacation plans or proposed projects for areas under their care. But that day was different. Very different. And I was not prepared for it. It made surrender a part of life in ways I had never seen it before.

Suzanne was in her fifties; she looked strong even though she had been sick for years, fighting a battle against death no one talked about and, in her case, fewer people could ever have surmised. She came from a farm family. They were hardworking people who had stayed on the land when the people around them moved to the city where the work was easier and the pay predictable. But they stayed on, harrowing and hoeing, through seasons of abundance and seasons of lean, taking each in equal stride.

Suzanne had been fighting her cancer for years in the same sure and steady, uncomplaining and commonplace way. But every year, the disease became more virulent and the drugs less effective. She had been shifted from doctor to doctor, from center to center until, by now, the treatments had reached the experimental stage.

By the time she asked to talk to me, she had already come to a new decision. "I want to stop the chemotherapy," she said to me. "The good times between treatments are getting shorter and shorter; the hard times are getting worse." I caught my breath. I talked to her about her meaning to the community, the model she was to all of us, about the value of her life to us. And then, seeing her quiet determination, I asked: "Why now, Suzanne? Why this great decision now? Why not see this last regime of chemotherapy through before making a decision like this?" She paused a moment. "It's almost Christmas time," she said. "The whole family comes home at Christmas time. I want the chance to say goodbye to everybody. Otherwise, I'll never see them all." I took a mental step back. "Come back in two weeks," I said. "Let's see how you feel about this then."

She was back to the day and the hour. "Suzanne," I said, "you realize the implications of this. There will be no turning back once you stop this program. Are you really sure about this?" Her answer was a simple one: "I have learned everything I can from these years," she said. "I'm ready." Suzanne died five months later. On my birthday. I took the lesson as gift.

There are times to let a thing go. There is a time to put a thing down, however unresolved, however baffling, however wrong, however unjust it may be. There are some things in life that cannot be changed, however intent we are to change them. There is a time to let surrender take over so that the past does not consume the present, so that new life can come, so that joy has a chance to surprise us again.

14. The Struggle of Vulnerability

W hen the Twin Trade Towers collapsed in downtown Manhattan,
it was hard to know what hurt the country most: that innocent
people lost their lives — or that the United States of America, the
greatest military threat in the history of the world, was itself vulnerable to attack. From the simplest of people. And with the simplest of
weapons — our own commercial airliners. The truth dawned: The
United States could be damaged. The United States was limited in the
world. We knew it and so did the rest of the world, all of whom slept a
little less soundly that night themselves. "If the United States is vulnerable, then what about us?" the fear implied.

It was an age-old lesson, long in coming. Vulnerability renders all
of us human, welcomes us into the human race, makes humanity an
unbreakable bond.

When Jacob wrestled with God, he must have wrestled as much
with the shock of being contested as he did with the strength of his foe.
After managing to survive the relentless demands of a sly and unscru-
pulous father-in-law, he was now plunged into a struggle that could
well limit his freedom forever. He was in dispute with something just as
strong, just as intent as he was and, this time, he was wounded by it. By
what, we're not sure. It may have been the specter of having to deal tomorrow with the brother he cheated years ago, or perhaps his own internal dis-ease with the consequences of his early life, the guilt that
comes with age. Or it may have been some kind of messenger from

God come to test his spiritual resolve. But whatever the nature of the opponent, it was a fearsome match. Jacob was not to get off easily here. "And Jacob's hip was dislocated as he wrestled with him," the story reads. It is fair warning to us all. Jacob did not escape scot-free, in other words. Struggle wounds us. It takes us down to size. It confronts us with the consequences of our limitations: We are not naturally superior to everything in life. We are all at base dependent. We will not always get our way. There will be things we cannot do in life.

When I withdrew my application from the creative writing program at Iowa State University, it was not with a sense of having been wronged. There was nothing unjust about the decision. Erratic, maybe. Groundless, perhaps. But not unjust. I was not losing anything I had a natural right to have. I was dealing with a sense of having been wounded, of having been limited, of having been stopped from becoming what I myself had decided I was that hung over the event like dark, dark fog.

It is one thing to be wronged, indeed. That's easy; in fact, it can be almost gratifying. It is another thing to be wounded. Wounded, our omniscient, almighty selves shrivel in the public eye. The two possibilities are easily confused but the effects of them are not. Dead, I am a war hero. Wounded, I am a loser. The Spartans of ancient Greece were very clear about the difference: "Better that a man be brought back on his shield rather than without it," they taught. It is one thing to be subjected to injustice and left to parade it. It is another thing entirely to be proven mortal. The humiliation of it singes our souls for years to come. The aftertaste of failure remains in the soul long after the rest of the world around us has forgotten the incident.

In the end, the United States' clash with terrorism wounded us as much or more psychologically than it cost us either in people or in places. It became an internal struggle of major proportions that struck at our sense of self, our stature in the world, our unassailable aplomb. Worst of all, it was a case of Gulliver finding himself at the mercy of Lilliputians, little people nowhere equal to the foe they had chosen. But in control, nevertheless. And therein lies the pain. The burden of humanity is the knowledge that at any time any one of us, all of us, may be brought down to size, defeated and left to bear it. The message of struggle is clear: No one, nothing, is totally invulnerable. Inside, all of us wage war with a sense of self that resists destructibility, defense-lessness and fragility with might and main.

Externally, nothing much changed after the fall of the Trade Towers. The country absorbed the shock and went on, in the words of President George W. Bush, by refusing to be stopped. We went back to work. We bought more stock. We shopped more than ever. We went on playing our national games. And we struck back ruthlessly, bombing other innocent people, twenty-four hours a day, sixty days in a row, trying to reclaim what the whole world now realized we also did not have: the aura of total invulnerability. So, whatever the ferocity of the counter-attack, in the back of the national mind, there was a lingering contusion. We, too, were mortal — but being mortal did not forgive us the obligation to go on.

To go on going on, in the face of repeated failures, despite being clearly damaged, in full view of a world that sees us to have been wounded, is to discover what it really means to be human. It is also the moment in which we are given the opportunity to reinvent ourselves, to become the rest of what we are able to be. Jacob, too, resisted with all his energy, and refused to let go, refused to give up. "Let me go," the stranger says. "It is almost dawn." I understand that. I myself went on writing in my little notebooks, never for a moment thinking I should stop, only that I would need to go about being who I was in a different way. But internally, the struggle to accept the fact that limitations are part of life raged on in me unabated.

To be less than perfect in a culture and an era that expects perfection rankles our sense of self. It puts into jeopardy all the unassail-ability we work so hard to imply. I have heard men who have come home to a burgled house say that the shock of it was worse than the loss of what had been taken. Pressed, one man said, "Now I know something about how a woman must feel when she's raped." It compares, in other words, to a violent encroachment on the private and pallid self. It is the awful proof that we are not as secure as we like to pretend we are, not as strong as we purport to be. It is living sign that no matter how impressive I see myself, there is always the possibility that I, too, may be vulnerable to forces I cannot see and do not know and cannot vanquish.

We have compassion for the handicapped but we find it uncomfortable to deal with them — not because we don't know what to do for them, as we insist, but perhaps because they remind us of how fragile, how limited we all really are in one way or another. They make naked all the weaknesses in ourselves that we most fear: that we, too, cannot really stand on our own two feet; that we, too, cannot sometimes see what's before our eyes; that we, too, cannot speak clearly enough what we wish we could say; that our souls, too, are twisted and confused and bowed down with the weight of living as are their bodies. This is a society of beautiful bodies and cosmetic surgery and anti-aging creams and health clubs. We run on treadmills because we do not run outdoors anymore. We diet because we do not control our eating habits. We use exercise bikes because we drive our cars everywhere. And in the end, we grow old anyway and fear to do so. Because we have put too much emphasis on the false perfection of fundamentally imperfect situations, we have overlooked those things in life that are really the ground of our truest strengths: the possibility of conversion, the call to independent thinking, faith in the presence of a companioning God, the courage to persist, surrender to the meanings of the moment, and a sense of limits that leads us to take our proper place in the human race.

Individuals who have no sense of their limitations fall hard when they fall. Nations that have no sense of their limitations crush others as they fall. The struggle to deny our vulnerabilities is the struggle to live a lie. It's not really difficult to determine how comfortable people are with their own limitations. It can be measured by the way they treat the limitations of others.

When we ignore the needs of the disabled or make them beg for the resources it takes to live a decent human life, when we deny them access to sidewalks, or ramps as well as stairs, or guide dogs in restaurants and hydraulic lifts on vans and voice recognition software on computers, when we hide them from the public arena, it is not a sign of their limitations. It is a sign of the singeing soul-sickness of ours. It means that we are at pains to hide from ourselves the very things that make us most human: our capacity to be wounded and the interdependence that requires of us.

My months in a polio hospital were some of the most devastating, most meaningful of my life. I was only sixteen when the disease struck and a life of unremitting disability seemed, on hard days, to be more than I could bear. No one knew if I would ever walk again. No one knew what, if anything, I would be able to do to make a living. No one could guarantee that I would get better. Nor did anyone try. And worse, whatever the sense of isolation, I was not alone in the dread and agony of polio's unknowables. Some people there, I realized — quarantined, bored by the interminable waiting for therapies and cures and help that never came — were more crippled by depression than by paralysis. Others railed daily at the thought of being restrained in any way. A few worked day and night to no avail against the ravages of the disease and got quieter and quieter as the months went by. But there were two fellows in the ward at the end of the hall who made all the difference: Every day at ten o'clock, just as the staff began to meet for consultations, they rolled from room to room in their wheelchairs organizing the daily wheelchair race in the hall. They gave points and prizes and long applause to the winners. It was weeks before I got up the energy to join them but when I look back now, I realize that the day I did was the day I began to get well.

Vulnerability is the call to self-acceptance. It is the great, liberating moment on the human journey.

15. The Gift of Limitations

⤫

It is a great burden to be perfect. The fear of failure skulks around the perimeters of hubris with irritating constancy. There is always the possibility that someone will come along who is even more perfect than we are. There is, if nothing else, the weight of being responsible for the world by those who think they are. Unable to accept ourselves as we are, we wear ourselves out in an effort to become unimpeachable.

Fortunately, we are spared the problems that come with perfection because none of us is. Not me; not you. It is, unfortunately, the strain of discovering the benefits of imperfection that takes so much time and effort in life. Every stage of life is a matter of trial and error. In each one there is something to be learned the hard way. The tendency is to approach them with naiveté, if not depreciation, and leave them with wisdom.

Erik Erikson, the great psychologist of personal development, is very clear about the crises we face at each stage of life and the need to complete each one successfully if the rest of life is to be satisfyingly healthy. It is to infancy that Erikson ascribes the task of learning trust. It is in infancy, he teaches, that the capacity for hope is born. The fact that even at the point of the weakest period of life our needs are met lays the foundation, he argues, for the notion that whatever our limitations, we will survive. That mothering figures respond to our cries, foresee our needs, tend to our helplessness, he says, provides the security it takes for the human being to tolerate insecurity.

But the task, however important, is seldom finished in childhood. Mothering figures themselves get sick, go away, become otherwise occupied, fail to hear us when we cry. And so we carry within ourselves always the possibility that there really is no one out there who will come when we call, no one who cares that we hurt, no one who will bring the bottle, arrange the covers, rock the cradle when we cry. The only alternative is to get control of the situation myself. The only alternative is to stay alert to the enemy, to be on the defensive against abandonment, to take charge, to become Fortress Joan. Mistrust and mastery, power and authority, domination and distance become the name of the game. I live to become sufficient unto myself, in charge of the world, invulnerable.

But then the fortress falls. The Trade Towers come down. The trusses of life begin to quiver. My Star Wars program is ineffectual. I am powerless and vulnerable, unsure and open to the elements of life, limited in resources and even more limited in spirit. Then my limitations can become my strength. Then I can discover the rest of the human race. Then I can come to realize the basic bounty of life. Then I am suddenly in a position to allow myself to be at the mercy of a merciful universe.

Jacob finds himself locked in bitter struggle, yes, but the foe that chastens him does not destroy him. He discovers that he is equal to the match but not superior to anything. He realizes that to trust in the benign intentions of another doubles his own strength.

It is, in fact, vulnerability to the strength of others that liberates us from the limits of the self. The ability to accept the fact, not only that we are limited but that limits are the very thing that make us valuable members of the human race, comes slowly in life. It is what we need but cannot supply for ourselves that makes us open to the rest of the world. It is what we have that the world needs that gives us any right to be part of the human community at all.

The paradox is that to be human is to be imperfect but it is exactly our imperfection that is our claim to the best of the human condition. We are not a sorry lot. We have one another. We are not expected to be self-sufficient. It is precisely our vulnerability that entitles us to love and guarantees us a hearing from the rest of the human race.

The definition of success in contemporary society is that a really

effective person takes up all the space there is everywhere, in everything: all the limelight, all the praise, all the money, all the power.
Ironically enough, in this most democratic of worlds, monarchy has
become the paradigm of success. Celebrities of every ilk — political,
corporate, or social — stand alone, by themselves, under the lights,
soaking up all the glitter, seldom surrounded by the hairdressers or
secretaries or agents or consultants who have made them look so
good. Superman and Wonderwoman are alive and well in a world that
fears vulnerability with a passion. But it is only vulnerability that pre-
pares us to live well, to understand others, and to take our proper place
in the human enterprise.

We have a sister in the community who has been in a wheelchair
since she was four years old. She is a victim of muscular dystrophy so
limiting that she moves only the thumb on her right hand. All day long
she sits in a body brace, her neck supported by a headrest, and "types"
letters to friends with the aid of voice recognition software. She doesn't
travel like the rest of us, or manage large institutions or organize workshops. But people flock to the monastery to talk with her — I think because they seem to know intuitively that in her powerlessness she understands theirs. It is this kind of sensitivity to the limits of the self that
his struggle taught Jacob and that the rest of us can take years to learn.

When going to a great university was denied to me, I learned what
it was to be third cook in a kitchen. I learned what I did not know. "Today, you'll have to make the sheet cake for lunch," the kitchen manager
said to me. "I will be making bread." I couldn't believe my ears. "But
how do I do that?" I said. "I've never cooked a thing in my life." She
was as incredulous as I was. "You're a bright girl. Read the directions,"
she said. I got up from the floor where I was scrubbing rubber marks
off the linoleum. "Sister Mary Ann," I said, "is there anything you
would like to know about the Civil War? Anything at all." I stood there
waiting, a slight smile on my lips, the truth of my inner poverty in my
eyes. The standoff was clear. She threw her head back and laughed.
"No," she said. "Not right now. But if I ever do, you'll be the first person I ask."

All of us wrestle with the angels of our inabilities all the time. We
live in fear that our incapacities will be exposed. We posture and eval-
uate and assess and criticize mercilessly. We insert ourselves into proj-

ects we know nothing about. We fail to allow others to love us for our weaknesses as well as for our strengths. Some of us spend time making ourselves imperious so that there will never be a doubt in anyone's mind who is the god of the day, the messiah of the moment, the king of the mountain, the goddess of heaven, the person in charge, the abbot, the boss, the president, the power. But down deep, that may be the most powerless position of all. If we refuse to ask for help, if we distance ourselves from the strengths of others, if we cling to the myths of authority and power where trust is needed, we leave out a piece of life. We condemn ourselves to ultimate failure because someday, somewhere, we will meet up with the thing we cannot do and our whole public self will depend on our being able to do it.

It is trust in the limits of the self that makes us open and it is trust in the gifts of others that makes us secure. We come to realize that we don't have to do everything, that we can't do everything, that what I can't do is someone else's gift and responsibility. I am a small piece of the cosmic clock, a necessary piece but not the only piece. My limitations make space for the gifts of other people. Without the grace of our limitations we would be isolated, dry, and insufferable creatures indeed. It is our limitations and the trust, the dependence on others, that springs from them that save us from all the tiny little deaths that struggle brings.

16. The Struggle of Exhaustion

It is not so much that struggle weaves itself in and out of every life that unnerves us. Defeat we understand, much as it may deflate us momentarily. Rather, it is the bone-sore, deep-down, heart-wearying, never-ending weight of struggles, the effects of which never go away, that wears us down and turns our spirits into dust. It is not the struggle itself that lays us low. It is the day-in, day-out tenacious clinging to the amorphous anger, the depression, the unacceptability of it all that stands to defeat us in the end. When a loved one dies, we survive the death. The only question is whether or not we will survive dealing with the death. When the divorce we did not want comes anyway, we survive the separation. The question is whether or not we will survive the thought of having been left. When work ends, we survive the retirement. It is finding ourselves useless that swallows us up day after day.

The story of Jacob's struggle with God is an interesting one. It is not the bruising that is emphasized in the telling of the story but the length of the struggle that is stressed. It is not that Jacob either held his own or was overpowered, was untouched or was hurt in the process that Scripture records, though it hints at all of them. What is underscored is that the struggle went on all night. In one short paragraph, the length of the contest is mentioned three times: "And there was one who wrestled with him until daybreak," the storyteller tells us. "Let me go, for day is breaking," the stranger says later. "The sun rose as he left Peniel," the story concludes.

Clearly, it is not that Jacob was or was not defeated by the stranger that is so much the point of the story as it is that he was exhausted by it. The struggle goes on, we realize, beyond the energy of anyone to endure it, evening through morning, from dusk till dawn, unendingly. Suddenly we understand why. Suddenly we come to see what we are being told: Exhaustion is the invisible enemy, the real enemy, in struggle. It's when we won't let go of a thing that we are defeated by it. "Let me go . . . ," says the Spirit of God. And Jacob answers, "I will not let you go until you bless me." And therein lies the secret of winning all the struggles of our lives. We must learn to let go of them so that we can come to the blessings hidden within them.

It's when we become fixated on a single vision of the future, the one we refuse to relinquish however clear its end, that struggle defeats us. To concentrate only on the struggle itself, to fail to force ourselves to understand what is meant to be discovered in this latest confrontation with the self, is to lose the things struggle is really meant to bring us. It's when we refuse to see that the struggle itself is some kind of blessing that we fail to best it in the end.

We like to define struggle as some kind of duel to the death with some mysterious, unknown, unjust, uncaring other. We like to keep scores, to talk in terms of who won and who lost. And no doubt, to some degree, those things matter. But in the end, it is what is going on within ourselves that determines what is really won or lost in the contest. In the end, it is the resolution of the combat within the self that counts. And exhaustion is the key to it.

The fact is that many of the things with which we struggle in life do themselves go on for years, if not for a lifetime. We struggle with envy and never quite manage to feel good enough about ourselves to get beyond it. We struggle with greed and never quite hoard enough things to satisfy us. We struggle with lust and confuse it with love. We struggle with jealousy and call it achievement. We struggle with love and in our intent to capture it manage to destroy it over and over again. We struggle with the circumstances of health or money or work or divorce and exhaust our hearts with the pain of them by refusing to live well within the boundaries of the life in which we find ourselves. It isn't that those things have not happened. It is that no one thing is the total definition of life for anyone.

At the end of summer camp, with nowhere to go, no university waiting, no writing career ahead, I went mechanically through the routine of class preparations for the upcoming teaching year. There was nothing I really wanted to do, no work I liked, no one to talk to with whom I could share my real feelings of deep depression and death of spirit. It was a very long and lonely time. All I could think of was what I had lost. All I could concentrate on was what I would not be able to be.

I could feel the exhaustion setting in. What was I doing here? How could I possibly stay in a place so dulling to my soul? Prayer helped, but prayer did not lift the pain or change the situation. Prayer simply reminded me that God was in the darkness with me, that I might be empty and hurting but that God was in the emptiness. God understood the pain, yes, but God did not change the pain. No, there was only one way to survive this and that was to find something that I could love as much as I loved what I had lost. Literature, I thought. I would read myself into oblivion. I would immerse myself in the writing of others until it seeped its way into my own soul, silently, unseen, unable to be taken away. I would begin to read myself into a world of beauty in the hope that beauty could sustain me through the ugliness of loss and that exhaustion would turn to energy again. And I did.

I read curriculum after curriculum that I set for myself: all the works of Shakespeare, all the American musicals, all the stories in the most definitive anthologies of American short stories. I simply read myself into a reason to get up the next day in order to read even more. And little by little I began to feel alive again.

Exhaustion is what happens when we refuse in our pain to look for ways to bring light into darkness. When we allow pain to consume us, to paralyze us, to nail our feet to the floor of the place where defeat has happened, danger sets in with a vengeance.

It is not struggle that destroys us. It is the unwillingness to move beyond struggle even when the struggle goes on forever. We don't forget the abandonment. We still feel the flames of jealousy. We still resent bitterly their new partner. We know we are divorced but refuse to be separated.

It is not the struggle itself that kills us. It is allowing ourselves to stay locked in mortal combat with it. The refusal to move on in life to where God waits for us with new love for new times breeds a desperation mired in a bog of denial. But desperation is meant to be a fuel, not an oppressive force that binds us to yesterday forever. "Desperation," wrote William Burroughs, "is the raw material of drastic change."[1] Desperation drives us to endure what we cannot change in order to become what we are next meant to be.

1. William Burroughs, *The Western Lands* (1987).

17. The Gift of Endurance

⬿

"There is no failure," Elbert Hubbard wrote, "except in no longer trying. There is no defeat except from within, no really insurmountable barrier save our own inherent weakness of purpose."[1] The words have the ring of truth to them. In fact, we see them being proven true every day of our lives. We are surrounded by people who struggle through terminal diseases and live years beyond any reasonable prognosis because they refuse to give up. They simply go on as if life were normal. They simply insist on living. We watch people fail at the professional dreams of life in one area and become great in areas they never dreamed they would ever attempt. There have been marathon runners who finished in the dark, long after the crowds had gone home, because finishing the race was more important to them than winning it. There is, in fact, no struggle that does not develop to the point where a person must choose between the fact of defeat and the effects of quitting.

Everyone is defeated sometime. Many then simply quit the fray. But the really strong, the really committed, do not. They decide instead whether or not the mountain is worth the climb. And if it is, no amount of wind can force them from the face of it. They endure for the sake of enduring. They live to finish what they began.

Endurance is not about being too stubborn to give up on the im-

1. Elbert Hubbard, *Elbert Hubbard's Scrap Book* (1923).

possible. Endurance is about having heart enough to keep on trying to do the possible, even if it is unattainable. We nurse the dying through years of disability. We begin projects for the poor even when they don't begin to make a dent in the problem of poverty. We hold on against opposition for the sake of the principle of a thing. Those endure who seek to do what is deeply important to them, no matter how difficult it may be.

The problem is that it is often hard to tell the difference between endurance and denial. It is a distinction that is necessary to the authenticity of the exercise. We are in denial when we fail to accept the fact that what we want to have happen depends on more than what we have to offer. If we do not have the basic musical abilities it takes to play a piano, no amount of music lessons will make up for the lack of natural rhythm or the size of our hands. Then, to set our sights on concertizing is denial. When we do not have the agreement of others that is needed to see a thing through but cling to it anyway, that is denial. I cannot save a marriage, for instance, once the other person has already left it. I cannot become what I set out to be when the resources do not exist yet that could make such a thing possible. I may be a paraplegic who wants to walk again, who struggles every day to get out of my wheelchair, but the neurological research necessary to such a medical advancement is still in the earliest stages of development. To continue to pursue what only those with adequately functioning legs can do, is denial. Endurance, then, does not mean "success." It means being willing to cope with what is until something else begins. It means being open to the possibility that things will stay the way they are, perhaps indefinitely. It means that I must begin to be open to becoming something new. Then, endurance demands that I bear what I must and be what I can.

The notion of endurance takes on negative overtones when I fail to realize that it is meant to bring out the best in me, not the worst. There is a kind of pseudo-endurance, a neurosis of the spirit, that warps our personalities and numbs our souls. We complain but we will not quit. We sulk but we do not change. We bear up but we do not enjoy. We miss the point entirely. We confuse endurance with sloth and drag our feet through life and expect the universe to thank us for the sacrifice we do not want to make. But endurance is not misery, not martyrdom, not spiritual machoism. Endurance means that I intend to survive the worst, singing as I go, knowing, as Jacob did, that "I have seen the face of God and survived."

Endurance is not gruesome. It is realistic. The one I love is dying and I care for them to the end with a love that never dies. But I care for them knowing that one day I will also begin to make a new future, not that I will be a perpetual victim of a love cut short by time gone bad. Endurance is what carries me through what I could otherwise never survive if I did not believe that it was eternally worthwhile to do so.

Endurance is not martyrdom. Only martyrdom is martyrdom. The person who endures does not have life taken away by forces devoted to their destruction. They lay it down of their own choosing. They devote their lives in tribute only to those things that make a life worth living. When my young widowed mother refused to allow other members of the family to raise her child so that "she could begin again," she was not martyring herself. She was simply intent on enduring the struggle it would take to keep alive and vital the only part of her life that still meant something to her: me. Endurance is not negation of life; it is commitment to whatever makes life worthwhile. It is the willingness to keep on doing what must be done because doing it is meaningful, is worthy of us, and more than equals the struggle it takes to do it.

Endurance is not an exercise in reckless machoism. It is not an adolescent attempt to prove that we can take pain. It is, in fact, a very feminine way to look at the world. It allows us to be committed and realistic at the same time. We do what we do, not because we are sure to succeed at it, but because it brings out something good in us that nothing else can touch. We can endure anything for the sake of the things we love. We can endure years at a bedside, years of study, a lifetime of practice, a career of service, the denial of good things we consider less worthy than the things we really care about. Endurance is the sacrament of commitment.

The gift of endurance is not to be wasted on trivia, on denial, on stubbornness, on posturing. We are given the gift of endurance for the sake of the great things of life, not for those pathetic little moments of paltriness that tempt us all, at first blush, to resist for the sake of resistance.

Endurance has as much to do with the kind of person we are as it has to do with the kind of situation we're in. In the words of Ralph Waldo Emerson, "What lies behind us and what lies before us are tiny matters compared to what lies within us."[2] What lies within us may be untested when what lies behind us and before us is unclear in consequence, uncertain in impact. But when there is no other choice I can make and know myself to be true to my best self, then endurance is of the essence.

Marguerite was the typical young wife of the time: educated in law, sophisticated in her interests, devoted to her husband and his burgeoning career. She lost her license to practice law by following him from one country to another but, no problem, she had other interests, broader ones, as well. She enrolled in a master's program in sociology that would take her beyond law, give her a wider arena in which to work, wherever, however, his career developed. But then the babies came. The birth of the first child interrupted the sociology degree; the birth of the second one in a second country interrupted the taking of the law exams. She was no longer a lawyer, then — just a person with a degree in law that was now essentially useless. And she was no longer a continuing student, either. But she never stopped reading.

She never for a moment gave up. She listened to the academic discussions around her dinner table. She attended every seminar, every discussion, every workshop she could. She prepared herself insatiably to go on learning. Finally, between running the house, ferrying the children, going the rounds of other people's meetings, hosting other people's parties, she entered a program in psychotherapy and opened her own counseling center. Then, at the age of forty-five, she re-began the master's program she'd missed twenty years before. At fifty, the children raised, the business flourishing, she finished a doctorate. It was not the way she had planned it. It was not what she set out to do. It was not easy. She would have done it differently if she could. But all that is beside the point. The point is that she did it at all. She endured. And in endurance found the limitless boundaries of her new, strong self, found the mettle of her soul.

I myself, cut off from a world of professional writers, went on writing in small notebooks I kept beside me in chapel until suddenly

2. Ralph Waldo Emerson, *The Essential Writings of Ralph Waldo Emerson* (2000).

they sprang to a new life of their own. And when other phone calls came over the years, telling me that I was not welcome by whomever to speak the truth as I saw it, to raise the questions I had, in various places, to various groups, I came to understand that it was the endurance of one life situation which, years later, enabled me to bear the other.

There is a capacity for endurance in the human heart. It persists even when every obvious avenue is closed. It beats with life even in the midst of death. It endures, not because there is no struggle to obstruct it, but because it is precisely the struggle itself that sharpens its focus, makes clear its real meaning.

Jacob is blessed for enduring a righteous struggle, not for winning it. It is doing what is worth doing, whatever the depth of the struggle that underlies it, which, in the end, is the gift.

18. The Struggle of Scarring

❧

"Good people are good," William Saroyan wrote, "because they come to wisdom through failure."[1] Struggle is the soul's ash heap of failure, of not being in charge, of not being on top, of not being sure that we will really survive this wrestling match with God by which we are being currently consumed. It starts the moment we realize that there is just the possibility that this time we may not manage to elude the forces of nature arrayed against us. We will not recover the money or the status or the security or the relationships we have come to take for granted.

When the phone call came that finished what I hoped would be my writing career before it had even begun, I saw no way out. Life seemed to end for me in mid-air. I was young enough to recover, I realize now, but time had no meaning then. The weight of despair that drained the energy out of my arms and legs was more, I was sure, than I would ever surmount in a lifetime. The struggle was how to live when there was little left for which to live. And, as a matter of fact, I did not really live again for a long, long time. I simply went on making well enough do, substituting summer school courses in a second-best degree for what had been the goal of my life, teaching high school students what I was not permitted to learn myself. It felt like inadequacy. It felt gray. It felt like death.

1. William Saroyan, New York *Journal-American* 23, August 1961.

Real struggle hurts. It marks us in ways we don't even always realize when it happens. Years can pass before we begin to comprehend the marks and scars trouble hews out of the flesh of our lives. It leaves us wounded and chastened and different for the rest of our days. "After he died," we hear a woman say, "I was never the same again." "When I didn't get the position," we hear a professional say, "it took the heart right out of me. I lost interest in everything." "When I couldn't go to college," we hear a young person say, "I stopped kidding myself that I'd ever be anything in life." "When we split up," we're told, "my life ended." Struggle brings us to crossover points in life after which we become new people, sometimes worse, often better, but always different.

We know things now that we never knew before. We know how meager is our imagination, how limited our vision. We know how small we can really be when we pit nobility of spirit against the comforts and the catering we want. We know how frightened we really are, how less-than-courageous we feel, how sniveling our sycophancy can really be. We know ourselves better than we ever did before. Most of all, we see life differently than we ever saw it before.

There is no hiding from struggle. It takes place deep down inside of us, in that tender place from which there is no refuge. No external enemy is nearly as demanding, as damaging, as destructive as the enemy within, the one of our own making. It is our own lust or pride or greed or jealousy or anger or gluttony or envy that takes us down. It is those against which we struggle. It is those that dog us from moment to moment, warring against the other forces within us, just as strong, just as intent, far more honorable. It is our innate compassion and humility and self-knowledge and largesse and justice and courage that call us to become our better selves. It is in the crucible of struggle that one of these outweighs the other, not always and not only, but often. In fact, is there anywhere other than struggle that they can really come to bloom?

It is when I finally settled down to be the best of what I could be where I was that I was finally ready to leave it. "When we yield to discouragement," Therese of Lisieux writes in her journals, "it is usually because we give too much thought to the past and to the future."[2]

2. St. Therese of Lisieux, *Peacemaking* (1989).

Only when we learn what the present is meant to teach us can we ever be ready — required — to move on from there.

Struggle shapes us and reforms us and shapes us again. It is the potter's kiln of life, the heat that creates the color and the quality of the glaze we call our years. But the heat of the potter's kiln also shrinks us down to size. "As much as a third the size of the original pot," Brother Thomas Bezanson, one of the major potters of the twenty-first century, shows me when I visit his workshop. And so it is with struggle. It burns off the dross of us, it fires us down to our real size and forces us to face the fact that whatever mightiness remains has more to do with the meaning of the struggle for us than with the manner of it.

There is no such thing as one struggle being more significant than another. Death is relief for some people, soul-searing for others. Poverty is crushing for some people, liberating for others. Work is a burden for some people, a blessing for others. It is not the nature of the struggle that counts. What counts is the effect of my particular struggle on me.

The spirit with whom Jacob wrestled, in the dark night, alone and powerless, injured him mightily. "Jacob limped," the scripture reads. He couldn't walk straight anymore. He lived forever marked by a remembrance of the night he wrestled with God. To go deep into the heart of ourselves, to grapple with the forces there that seek to own our souls, to run the risk of losing to our smaller, narrower selves, exacts a toll, requires a ransom, demands that a price be paid.

We diminish the notion of struggle when we talk about "struggle" but mean "difficulties." Struggle is never done without cost. Real struggle marks us for life. It is a battle that is forever seething in the depths of us. It cannot be smoothed over. It can never be undone. We will bear its imprint forever in the face of our souls. The woman who comes to say of herself always, "My name is Ellen and I am an alcoholic," knows the meaning of the one inside who wrestles with us and is never entirely subdued. Sometimes it leaves us fearful, less arrogant, more open to others. Sometimes it leaves us timid, less cocksure, more respectful of others. Sometimes it leaves us angry, more self-critical, less naive. Sometimes it leaves us shamed. Whatever the wound on the soul with which struggle marks us, it leaves us limping. We limp forever to remind us, not that we are weak, but that inside us lies the

strength, if only we hold on long enough, if only we endure, to struggle and to survive. "Jacob prevailed," the scripture reads. Jacob out-
lasted the siege. Jacob lived to wrestle with God another day, as do we
all, for struggle is not singular and it is not an end. It is the nature of
life and it signals always the possibility of a new beginning.

19. *The Gift of Transformation*

Struggle changes us; it grows us up. It takes the dew off the rose and the gilt off the silver. It turns the fantasies of life into reality. But struggle does more than that. It also gives life depth and vision, insight and understanding, compassion and character. It not only transforms us, it makes us transforming as well. Then we become equal to the pressures of the world around us. Once we have truly struggled with something that stretches the elastic of the spirit, we are worthy to walk with others in struggle, too. Then we're ready to listen. Then we're able to lead. When we know the meaning of what it is to struggle with something in life we become totally human.

When we find ourselves immersed in struggle, we find ourselves trafficking in more than the superficial, more than the mundane. That's why maturity has very little to do with age. That's why wisdom has more to do with experience than it does with education. We begin to feel in ways we could never feel before the struggle began. Before a death of someone I myself have loved, someone else's grief is simply a formality. We don't know what to say and we don't know why we're saying it because we never needed to have someone say it to us. Before feeling humiliated ourselves we can never know how painful the daily paper can be to those who find themselves in it with no way to defend themselves to the great faceless and anonymous population out there that is using it to judge them. Silently, harshly, even gleefully, perhaps. Until my own reputation is at stake, I can look at another person's shame and never have the grace to turn away.

After we ourselves know struggle, we begin to weigh one value against another, to choose between them with the future, rather than simply the present, as our measure. Everything ceases to be equal. One thing is not as good as another. Some things, often quite common things, we come to realize — peace, security, love — are infinitely better than the great things — the money, the position, the fame — that we once wanted for ourselves. Then we begin to make different kinds of decisions.

We begin to see beyond the present moment to the whole scheme of things, to the very edges of the soul, to the core of what is desirable as well as what is doable. The bright young man who had worked the pit in the futures market, planned a big international career in trading, and worked hard to start his own business, changed jobs after the collapse of the World Trade Center. He stood in shock a thousand miles away as television cameras watched the building go down with dozens of his friends in it. All of them young, like he was. All of them bright, like he was. All of them on their way up, like he was. But to where? He had lost too many of his hard-driving young friends, he said later — all of whom, it had once seemed, were even more successful than he was — to ignore the meaning of life any longer. He quit his job in the center of Bigtime. He went back home to Smalltown, USA, to hunt his dogs and fish the streams and buy the average family home in a small cul-de-sac in a local suburb.

No one comes out of struggle, out of suffering, the same kind of person they were when they went in. It's possible, of course, to come out worse than we were when we went into the throes of pain. Struggle can turn to sour in us, of course. But it is equally possible, if we choose to reflect on it, to come out stronger and wiser than we were when it began. What is not possible, however, is to stay the same.

Struggle is the great crossover moment of life. It never leaves us neutral. It demands that we make a choice: either we dig down deep into the wellspring that is our innermost selves and go on beyond where we were, despite where we were, or we simply give up, stop in our tracks rooted to the spot, up to our ankles in bitterness and despair, satisfied to be less than all our personal gifts indicate that we are being called to be.

My mother could have given me away to the sister of hers who wanted to raise me. She had every opportunity to do so, after all. And it was certainly the smarter thing to do. She would have been more marriageable had she done it. She could have started all over again without me. After all, she was young and pretty and I was too little to know the difference. Instead, she decided that we would start all over again together. And in her transformation, she transformed me as well. I learned by watching her something I could never have learned simply by hearing about it: I learned that struggle tempers the steel of the soul. It straightens the backbone and purifies the heart. It makes demands on us that change us forever and makes us new. It shows us who we are. Then we make choices, maybe for the first time in life, that determine not only what we'll do in life but what kind of person we'll be for the rest of it.

The Roman philosopher Seneca said of struggle, "Failure changes for the better, success for the worse." Success can soften us but there is in struggle a challenge to those parts of us that cannot come fully to life except in the darkness of adversity. Courage, character, self-reliance, and faith are all forged to a fine point in the fire of affliction. We wish that it were otherwise. We rail and fuss because it's not. But the fact is that there are simply some parts of the human character that are honed best, and maybe only, under tension. Nothing else demands so much of us. Nothing else unmasks us to ourselves to the same degree. Nothing else exorcises the self-centeredness in us to the same degree. It teaches us our place in the universe. It teaches us how little we really need in life to be happy. It teaches us that every day life starts over again.

After the writing career I had hoped to pursue had been made impossible, but still desperate to write, to work with words, to find an outlet for the ideas that plagued me from morning to night, I began to find fiction in reality rather than reality in fiction. I began to become aware of the human stories in front of me that really counted. I began to be sensitive to the effects of the world around me on actual people around me. I ceased to make up stories and began to understand the stories of people I saw every day: I saw hard-working Mrs. Petulla,

who in her seventies went on cleaning houses and cooking other people's dinners for them every day because women never received a husband's entire social security check. And I began to write about inequality. I saw an African-American friend refused service in a
restaurant, not directly, just subtly: there was no table "available" for
me as long as I was with her. I began to write about racism. I saw more
and more families given flags instead of sons as a useless, winless war
in Vietnam raged on at the expense of families on both sides of the di-
vide. I began to write about social justice issues. I saw women under-
educated, unemployed, and underpaid, as my mother had been, and
began to write about the role of women in society. I saw women beg
for the bread at the altar of our churches and be denied. I began to
write about the conflict between theology and the gospel. I didn't need
to make up a story to tell it. I was living in the midst of stories everywhere.

I watched how all those people changed and prevailed, prevailed
and changed, as Jacob did. "Your name shall no longer be Jacob but Is-
rael," the story tells us. "Because you have been strong against God,
you shall prevail against many." When we prevail, in other words, we
are transformed. We become someone with a gift to give to others on
the way. And I prevailed and was transformed, as well. I began to understand that I wasn't called to write fiction; I was called to speak the
pain of reality. I, like everyone who ever lived, was being transformed
for the sake of being transforming. For me, it meant learning to give
the voiceless a voice. My new name, I came to understand, was truth,
not fiction.

20. Wrestling with God

Jacob, wounded, exhausted, confused, and struck down in the dark, emerges from his experience a chastened but stronger person. He has confronted everything life has to offer and prevailed. He hasn't given in. He hasn't given up. He has struggled to hold his own against forces far superior to himself. He has kept on trying. He has struggled till dawn. And finally he has been able to name the place where the struggle happened "Peniel," which in Hebrew means, "I have seen the face of God and survived."

It's a poignant moment in the history of spirituality. In the end, the story implies, the spiritual life is not simply a matter of doing good works or practicing the social virtues or earning a good reputation or living a life of religious regularity. What is needed is reconciliation with the world around us. Jacob had stolen from his brother, deceived his father, run away from almost certain punishment for those things, and, in the end, tricked his father-in-law in order to secure his own fortune. But he has wrestled with all of it and prevailed. He has faced himself and all his weakness. He has come home to himself, open to tomorrow, ready to begin all over again. He has begged God for blessing and trusted in its coming. Jacob has hope, hard-won and real.

Jacob does what all of us must do if, in the end, we, too, are to become true. He confronts in himself the things that are wounding him, admits his limitations, accepts his situation, rejoins his world, and goes on. It's not easy, of course, but it is the confrontation with the self

87

that gives both depth and texture to life. Without it, we can predict behavior but we can never completely understand it, not even when it is
our own. Only when we face despair, only when we give in to the limits
of the self, do we know the tenor of our faith. Only when we deal with
depression do we begin to be able to measure the quality of hope that
is in us to carry us through all the dark spots of our lives.

Western civilization, and the United States in particular, has developed to the point where pain is unacceptable, headaches are some
kind of affront to human development, strain is a problem to be
solved, stress is intolerable. On the public front, technology promised
us peace, psychology promised us personal health, social psychology
guaranteed us group success, medicine teased us with promises of
eternal youth, bionic regeneration, and well-being. No wonder, then,
that we feel frustrated and fearful in the face of so many wonder drugs,
medical and otherwise, that have disappointed us. With the largest,
most powerful military the world has ever known, we are living in
more fear than ever before. With all the encounter groups in the world,
we are also dealing with more divorce than society has ever known.
With all the scientific wonders of the Western world, we still suffer
from diseases no one ever knew we had. We still get sick. We still die.

The promises have failed us. The expectations remain. No wonder
then that we flee from relationships that require something of us to
maintain them, regardless how fundamental, regardless how benign
they may be. No wonder we strike out when we're confronted. No
wonder we become despondent when what we want we do not get. We
go to psychologists to fill up the emptiness and calm our fears. We beg
psychiatrists for medicine to blunt the hurts within us, even when the
hurts are not medical in origin. We lose sight of the fact that hurt may
actually be part of the process of life. We fail to understand that the
pain we feel may be more of the spirit than of the psyche, more of the
soul than of the chemistry of the mind.

Wrestling with God is of the essence of life. In the process we
learn things about the self and we come to understand some things
about God as well. Given enough struggle, it becomes very clear after
a while: God is not a puppeteer. God is not a magician. Our lives lie in
our own hands and we will have to take charge of them before anything important about them can really come to resolution. Struggle is

the process that drives us to find God within us and in the darkness that surrounds us.

When we talk about the spirituality of struggle, we need to talk about every part of the process. Spiritual recovery is not a quick-fix solution. A young cousin of mine with an Eagle Scout rating to his credit, a college education at his fingertips, a new baby, a beautiful wife — everything in the world to live for — committed suicide. No one knows what the issue was that led to such despair but one thing we know for sure: it was the loss of something he felt he could not do without. No technology makes up for the wantings of the human soul. No promises of living happily ever after will substitute for the internal awareness it takes to live without what will not last forever in the first place.

Struggle is not one thing; it is many things. It's not simply an event, a happening, a disappointment. It is all the internal processes that accompany a blow to the psyche so momentous, so sudden, so unexpected, so unwanted that there is no way whatsoever to prepare for its coming. The struggle that threatens to take us down into the pit of life is whatever we cannot imagine living without — money or status or love or acceptance or security or public approval or things. Why? Because at any moment, those things can and will be taken away. And at the moment any of them go, we discover both who we are and who we must become if we are ever to be able to live life fully alive. Not simply going through the motions. Not simply breathing. Not simply robotized.

Struggle forces us to confront our illusions both about the world and ourselves. It requires us not simply to seek hope but to become hope ourselves. It urges us to move beyond the cages that entrap us in the past in order to live with new imagination. Whatever we loved and lost in the past is the best proof we have that life can be good in the future if we will only make it so within ourselves.

Hope is greater than faith because hope not only believes in the presence of the God of Eternity. Hope believes, as well, in the God of Time who companions us now and waits for us in a beneficent future as we discover in struggle all the layers of life within us that go basically unseasoned in times of plenty but wax in times of lean.

Struggle is, in other words, the gift of new life in disguise. A hard gift, perhaps. A strong gift, indeed. But a gift without which we run the risk of going to our graves only half alive.

The twelfth-century Persian poet Jalaluddin Rumi put it this way:

> I saw Grief drinking a cup of sorrow
> and called out,
> "It tastes sweet,
> does it not?"
> "You've caught me," Grief answered,
> "And you've ruined my business.
> How can I sell sorrow
> when you know it's a blessing?"[1]

It isn't that struggle is something to be prescribed. It is not a matter of recommendation. That attitude is commonly called masochism, the sick satisfaction a person gets from self-abuse. But struggle is something which, in order to be spiritually whole, we must learn to wrestle with and deal with well for the sake of the expansion of our own small souls. It gives salt to life. In our struggles we come to understand, to taste deeply the rest of life. Helen Keller, the woman struck both deaf and blind who not only learned to communicate herself but taught others to do so as well, wrote, "The hilltop hour would not be half so wonderful if there were no dark valleys to traverse."

There is beauty in the dark valleys of life. It is called hope.

---

1. Rumi, Quatrain no. 1707. Trans. Coleman Barks (1993).

21. The Process of Struggle

When I sat on the banks of the creek at camp, grieving the loss of the dream of my life, I was as frightened as I was disconsolate. Something was happening to me that had never happened before. I had somehow lost control of myself. One moment things seemed relatively normal. I talked to people, functioned well, went about my business, not with great joy but with at least a sense of purpose. I didn't like what I was doing but I was doing it. No one knew the hurt. I talked to no one about the loss. I simply went on going on. But, suddenly, without warning, in the very next moment, I would find myself swimming in a sea of black, my arms and legs heavy and lifeless, tears in my eyes. The frustration of it all swept over me like waves on a beach, pulling me under, upending me in deep water, washing me out away from a firm emotional shore. Day after day, the struggle raged. I wanted to quit; I couldn't quit; there was an obvious reason to leave if I were not fitted for the place; there were reasons larger than the writing I would now never do that begged me not to quit. This was, I told myself, part of the sanctifying sacrifice of the life that I myself had chosen by the very act of entering a monastery in the first place. But what was the good of staying if I could only pull myself through from dawn to dark by dint of sheer willpower alone every day for the rest of my life, if the sacrifice was not a willing one? And was sacrifice that was some sort of distortion of the person what God was all about? What religious life was all about? Why stay and be unhappy — underdeveloped —

forever? Did "sacrifice" mean the loss of the self, and if so, what did that have to do with the God of creation? At what point did acceptance become blasphemy?

The process of struggle is the process of the internal redefinition of the self. People do it in the midst of a marriage that is failing on one set of expectations and in need of being renegotiated around others. People do it when the work they do ceases to be for them what they expected it to be. People do it when they find themselves locked out socially of the very places they want to be in life: in the midst of the dominant culture, in a position of power and authority, in a place of comfort and security. When our expectations run aground of our reality, we begin to rethink the meaning and shape of our lives. We begin to rethink not just our past decisions but our very selves. It is a slow but determining deconstruction of the self so that a real person can be reborn in us, beyond the expectations of others, even beyond our own previously unassailable assumptions. And struggle is its catalyst.

Struggle is a process, not an event. It follows a cycle which, if not recognized, stands to embroil us in unfinished emotions forever, but which if resolved frees us to go on even stronger than we were before it happened. Struggle is always an invitation to a new life that, the longer it is resisted, the longer we fail to become who we are really meant to be. The stories of people trapped in the past — the ones for whom the story of their past struggle has become the story of their present grief, their living anger, their unfinished definitions of themselves — are the stories of people who were never able to complete the cycle of liberation, the odyssey of hope.

The Hebrew Testament story of Jacob wrestling with God is a model of the process. It is given to us to apply like a template to our own lives. Each element of the small vignette is a warning call to us to attend to what God is allowing to happen to us here and now so that we might go on even healthier in times to come. It provides a series of checkpoints for the spiritual life. It is in itself a veritable spirituality of struggle, which exposes to us those elements of suffering that call us to growth and give us new life. It includes within itself eight phantoms of the soul that expose to us those aspects of life that are yet beyond our spiritual grasp:

Change

Jacob is a happy man when the incident happens. He is at the point at which it seems that everything in life is finally perfect for him. He is financially secure, married to the woman he pursued for years, self-assured and destined to inherit the family fortune. He's on the brink of great success.

But that is precisely the point. Struggle always happens just when it seems that we have everything we ever wanted just the way we always wanted it. It is a sudden, unforeseen interruption of our perfect lives, the thing we thought would never happen to us, the reversal of a fortune we deserve, the loss of what we had worked hard to achieve. The change is psychologically cataclysmic, out of time, unacceptable.

Isolation

Jacob is alone when the struggle begins. There is not a soul around to whom he can talk about it. There is no one who can even give him comfort, let alone aid. He's in this alone. And that is the point. It is the isolation of struggle that wears us down. If we show our pain, we may be mocked for it, or ridiculed for it, or gloated over because of it. If we fail to show our pain, it stands to smother us even as we go on smiling.

Darkness

Jacob is assailed at night, the scripture says — as he goes to sleep, apparently. And in the darkness he finds himself in a struggle. Just as surely as there is some kind of physical duress in the experience, it is even more a struggle of great internal proportions. His soul is caught in a tangle of motives and desires that threaten to consume him, or even to destroy him.

In darkness of spirit we each wrestle with feelings that threaten to overwhelm us. We wrestle with the sense of indignity that comes with finding ourselves in circumstances in life that we know are beneath us, with the anger that comes from losing, with the feeling of abandonment that comes with being left to fend alone at the hardest moments of life, with the emotional wreckage that is the detritus of injustice. In the center of ourselves, we begin to come apart.

Fear

Jacob fears that he is losing the battle to save himself. He is barely able to hold on, let alone to triumph over a foe he does not understand and cannot name.

The fear of losing everything we ever worked for, ever lived for, becomes all-consuming. The past is gone, it seems, and any kind of decent future is impossible. Fear runs cold through the heart and paralyzes the spirit.

Powerlessness

Jacob comes to know what it is to be ineffective, impotent, helpless. After years of success, now without warning, suddenly, in an instant, everything he has come to be is gone. He is no longer powerful, omnipotent, in charge — not even of himself.

But that is the storm of struggle: to be lost in a maelstrom that is not only not of our own making but also beyond our control is its essence. If we did not grasp so tightly, it would not be so difficult to let go, true, but in the end it is not the grasping that is the problem. It is the inability to relax, to detach, to disengage long before this present debacle that takes us down. We have centered our lives in impermanence and failed to call it fleeting. We make one thing the definition of the self and when it goes, the core of us goes with it.

Vulnerability

Jacob discovers, in the course of his struggle, that not only is he powerless to prevent the situation but he is vulnerable to it, able to be broken by it. He suddenly realizes that he has been wounded. The long, hard effort to maintain his balance, to continue the contest against his fear, to avoid going down into the black darkness forever has sapped his strength and left him weak.

We know the situation all too well. It is the part of struggle that attacks our very sense of self. We who once thought ourselves to be invincible are now left to the whims of the winds around us. We are felled and it is the being made fallible that is the greatest sting of all.

Exhaustion

Jacob wrestles the whole night long, until dawn. Jacob, in other words, is exhausted by it all. He wants to quit but doesn't. He wants to name his danger, understand it, but can't. He wants a blessing out of it in the worst way. He wants to make sense of the whole thing but there is no sense to be had. What he worked so diligently to achieve, he may never secure. What he wanted, he will not get. What he values most in life is in danger. And he doesn't even know why.

Exhaustion may be the greatest enemy of all, we know. When we work for years at something, only to see it begin to fail when we ourselves have little energy left to begin again, is the hardest part of the process, perhaps. It is Sisyphus reborn. We spend years beginning and beginning and beginning again to reach the peak of our aspirations, and in the space of a moment, it crumbles at our feet.

Scarring

Finally, Jacob is bandied, impaired, crippled. He walks into the struggle but he limps out of it, permanently marked, forever changed, ever limited by the experience. But scarring as struggle may be, we also know down deep that it vitalizes another whole part of us. Our sensibilities reach a higher tone. We become a fuller self.

It is precisely in the course of responding to each part of the cycle of struggle — to change, isolation, darkness, fear, powerlessness, vulnerability, exhaustion, and scarring — that hope emerges, takes our hearts captive, and leads us on. It is, ironically, the very process of responding with determination to each element in struggle that itself nourishes hope. It is the very act of resisting despair that abolishes despair.

The spirituality of struggle is, then, a spirituality that takes change and turns it into conversion, takes isolation and makes it independence, takes darkness and forms it into faith, takes the one step beyond fear to courage, takes powerlessness and reclaims it as surrender, takes vulnerability and draws out of it the freedom that comes with self-acceptance, faces the exhaustion and comes to value endurance for its own sake, touches the scars and knows them to be transformational.

Out of all these things comes new strength and a new sense of self, new compassion and a new sense of the purpose of life. It is struggle that is the foundation of hope, not hope that is a hedge against struggle.

22. The Process of Hope

Hope is rooted in the past but believes in the future. God's world is in God's hands, hope says, and therefore cannot possibly be hopeless. Life, already fulfilled in God, is only the process of coming to realize that we have been given everything we need to come to fullness of life, both here and hereafter. The greater the hope, the greater the appreciation of life now, the greater the confidence in the future, whatever it is.

But if struggle is the process of evolution from spiritual emptiness to spiritual wisdom, hope is a process as well. Hope, the response of the spiritual person to struggle, takes us from the risk of inner stagnation, of emotional despair, to a total transformation of life. Every stage of the process of struggle is a call to move from spiritual torpor to spiritual vitality. It is an invitation to live at an antipodal depth of soul, a higher level of meaning than the ordinary, the commonplace generally inspires. The spirituality of struggle gives birth to the spirituality of hope.

Conversion

Unwanted change — the only kind of change that is real, if the ancients are to be believed — requires more than simply a transition from one state or stage of life to another. It requires conversion of heart. It requires acceptance. It demands that we be willing to believe that where we find ourselves now, bad as it may seem, must be at least as good — at least eventually — as where we ourselves wanted to be. Conversion assumes an openness to the God of creation, of newness, of wonder and surprise.

Conversion takes us far beyond our childhood God of Law. The problem is that we too often reduce our relationship with God to a set of rituals and exercises, rules and requirements, which only the brave dare to question, few want to deal with, and most simply take as the ultimate in the spiritual life. We look for perfection in a totally imperfect world. More, like children trying to please a parent into granting permission, we bargain with God. If we ourselves are perfect, we decide, God will bless us and free us from evil. So, when we finally get things right, meaning when we finally get things as we want them to be, we simply do not want to start over again. We begin to doubt a God who is not a vending machine. Conversion is the first step to a mature faith. It is the willingness to start over again, to admit that things are not finished, to know that this is a God because of whom creation never ceases and growth never ends. Conversion, then, is the first stage in the flowering of hope.

Independence

Isolation, the aloneness that comes when we are left locked in dreams left empty by change, calls us to hope in a companioning God. When friends and family, caring onlookers and competent professionals disappear, we are left to our own devices to face the consequences of the cataclysms of our life. When everyone else, become uncomfortable in the face of pain they cannot cure, either has disengaged themselves from our misery or remains so foreign to it that everything they say to comfort only widens the gap between us and the rest of the human race, loneliness drains us of whatever strength we might have left. Then, we begin to realize that it is we who must begin to reach out again. It is we who must begin to talk about other things. It is we who must begin to think about other things. We must find within us the will to grieve and to live at the same time. We must become independent of our own pain. To curl up within the pod of the self and cry is to deny hope. But to insist on living even when we feel dead inside is hope come to life.

Faith

The dark night of the soul, that feeling of abandonment by God in the midst of great and total need, can bring us to the very edge of sanity. More than one person has gone over that edge into blackness and never recovered. The feeling is a strange, tormenting one, perhaps, to those for whom life seems good right now but perfectly understandable to those for whom it is not. To feel marooned in the universe without a soul to depend on, they argue, makes life for them a useless exercise. They literally see nothing that, at the present time, makes life worth living.

Faith, on the other hand, that early notion that life is bigger than we are, that there is something out there that is eternally just, eternally loving, is the antidote to darkness and a strong step in the exercise of hope. Life is obviously good. Psalmists relied on it in the midst of their own despair millennia ago: "You cause the grass to grow for the cattle," Psalm 104 reminds us, "and plants for people to use to bring forth food from the earth, and wine to gladden the human heart, oil to make the face shine, and bread to strengthen the human heart." Faith is far more than wishful thinking. We have proof. An act of faith is the beginning of hope. It casts our own small needs into the arms of a God who has provided for the needs of the universe. Surely there is hope for us.

Courage

When fear of the unknown strangles the heart, one tiny act of courage can bring hope alive — frail and sputtering, perhaps, but there to be grasped in the midst of the emptiness. One small attempt to find a new job, one night out with a new friend, one open and honest talk with a good listener, one signed petition, one question spoken in the face of its silencers, one foray into one place we have never been before — the art gallery, the group meeting, the concert, the new library, a day of fishing — are all small human acts that take courage when we would rather lie cowering in our bed. But hard as they may be, little as we may care about them at the time, they put us back in control of life, meager as it may then look, empty as it may feel. Tiny acts of courage are tiny acts of hope.

Surrender

Powerlessness is not a modern virtue. The people of our age — that is, *we* — are not easily obsequious, no matter who we are. We take class-lessness seriously, much as it does not really exist. We are persons with some kind of power, we insist, however fanciful, however much a myth. We seriously think we have rights and voice and place. It's a strange contradiction. In this world of megacorporations and global networks and nuclear threat and invisible international links, the individual has never been so assertive — and never been so powerless.

Life is, for the most part, out of our control. We boast about democratic participation and watch votes discarded in national elections at the whim and fancy of a few. We glory in the impregnability of our national defense system and watch the economic center of the country go down in minutes under the blow of two commercial airliners, our own, while we stand helplessly by. We see rivers clog up and air go gray and land go to dust around us and there's not a thing we can do about it. Then we turn on our television sets and realize that someone, in the name of justice and on our behalf, is now raining down another kind of terror on other innocent people half a world away.

Then only surrender is possible. But not the kind of surrender that gives over conscience and humanity to the inhumanity of others. We must now surrender to the obligation to understand and to care. We must surrender ourselves to becoming conscious, thinking members of the human race. We must put down the temptation to powerlessness and surrender to the questions of the moment.

It is not a matter of changing what cannot be changed. It is a matter of refusing to allow what ought to be changed to conform us to itself. Perhaps there is nothing we can do but surrender ourselves to pursuing the question of why it is that now in this great and glorious world nothing can be done for those whose lives are dismally inglorious. That alone would be an act of hope to many and a spark of hope in my own soul. It would tell me that I am still alive, that my soul at least has not died at the hands of the culture of death around me.

Limitations

It is one thing to be powerless. Powerlessness I can sometimes ignore in the name of indifference. If I am simply unaffected by something, disdainful of it, uncaring, then I cannot be hurt by it. But if it means something to me. If it exacts a price from me. If I can be limited by it. If I am vulnerable to it in any way whatsoever, then it is another thing entirely.

To admit that I am wounded, to have it be known that I am weak, to know that I myself can be — *am* — bridled by something ices the blood in my veins. To be constrained by anything, to find myself reduced to size and unmasked in my arrogance by the power of something greater than myself — a system, a disease, a situation not of my own making — is a galling, despairing moment. Then I must choose between flailing in the face of the inevitable or admitting that my ability to accept my limitations, to depend on the strengths of others, is the only hope I have. It is the long delayed awareness that, whatever my own weaknesses, I do not need to fall.

Hope lies in the gifts and giftings of others. "In my weakness is my strength," St. Paul said. I come to know the truth of the statement. In the acceptance of my limitations is my hope for salvation from what I cannot handle alone and need not try. In those very limitations is the beginning of my hope that God, working in others, will be the strength I need.

Endurance

There is a deep-down bone weariness that comes with struggle. The sheer weight of going on knowing that nothing we can do will change things as they are, that there is no going back to what was, exhausts the timbre of the soul. We want to give up. We want to quit. We want to give in to the thing that has defeated us and die. But the very fact that we do not succumb to the weariness of the impossible, that we endure, that we keep on keeping on touches into the hope of eternal justice, eternal good, everlasting possibility. Then we see that our creating God who goes on creating — whatever the apparent failures of the process — asks the same of us. When we refuse to give up, either on ourselves or on the world around us, we become our own small sign that God is, that in the end right will prevail, that hope lives. Endurance is the light of hope in a continuing darkness that must somehow, somewhere give way to the light of Jacob's dawn.

Transformation

The important things in life, one way or another, all leave us marked and scarred. We call it memory. We never stop remembering our triumphs. We never stop regretting our losses. Some of them mark us with bitterness. But all of them can, if we will allow them, mark us with wisdom. They transform us from our small, puny, self-centered selves into people of compassion. For the first time, we understand the fearful and the sinful and the exhausted. They have become us and we have become them as well. We recognize the down-and-out in the street who mirrors our despair. We commiserate with the anger of the marginalized. We identify with the invisibility of the outcast. We can finally hear the rage of the forgotten. We are transformed.

Then and only then can the world really have hope that we ourselves are worth having hope in. Then and only then can we take back our power, break the barrier of isolation, transcend our limitations, find the hope in ourselves that emerges out of struggle, that refuses to give in to despair, that lives only in us.

Struggle is a cycle that threatens to splinter our souls into shambles. Hope is the legacy that emerges in response to each of struggle's deceptions that change is destructive, that we are alone, that God has deserted us, that we are unequal to the task, that we cannot go another step, that our scars have left us forever unfit.

Despair is a spiritual disease into which is built its antidote: hope. It is a matter of refusing to die at exactly the moment when we are being offered new life.

Hope is not a denial of reality. But it is also not some kind of spiritual elixir. It is not a placebo infused out of nowhere. Hope is a series of small actions that transform darkness into light. It is putting one foot in front of the other when we can find no reason to do so at all.

A Native American tale tells of the elder who was talking to a disciple about tragedy. The elder said, "I feel as if I have two wolves fighting in my heart. One wolf is the vengeful, angry, violent one. The other wolf is the loving, compassionate one." The disciple asked, "But which wolf will win the fight in your heart?" And the holy one answered, "It depends on which one I feed."

The spiritual task of life is to feed the hope that comes out of despair. Hope is not something to be found outside of us. It lies in the spiritual life we cultivate within. The whole purpose of wrestling with God is to be transformed into the self we are meant to become, to step out of the confines of our false securities and allow our creating God to go on creating. In us.

23. The Gift of Hope

⁓

"Hope," the fantasy writer Margaret Weis wrote, "is the denial of reality."[1]

I completely disagree.

Reality is the only thing we have that can possibly nourish hope. Hope is not based on the ability to fabricate a better future; it is grounded in the ability to remember with new understanding an equally difficult past — either our own or someone else's. The fact is that our memories are the seedbed of our hope. They are the only things we have that prove to us that whatever it was we ever before thought would crush us to the grave, would trample our spirits into perpetual dust, would fell us in our tracks, had actually been survived. And if that is true, then whatever we are wrestling with now can also be surmounted.

Hope lies in the memory of God's previous goodness to us in a world that is both bountiful and harsh. The God who created this world loves it and us in it, but at the price of our own effort, at the cost of our own craving for more of the vision, more of the depth, more of the truth of the life. The God who made this world has blessed it with good things, yes — but all of them take working at: coconuts need to be cracked, soil needs to be tilled, mountains need to be climbed, water needs to be conserved. God does not do this for us. God simply

1. Margaret Weis, *Dragons of Winter Night* (1985).

companions us as we go. God has given us in this unfinished world a glimpse of eternity and walks with us through here to there, giving us possibility, giving us hope.

The proofs of eternal rebirth are everywhere. Spring comes every year. Dawn comes every morning. Love happens out of hate. Birth absorbs the pain of death. And people everywhere look to Nirvana, to enlightenment, to reincarnation, to resurrection in the hope of eternal renewal. To the Christian, both the crucifixion and the resurrection of Jesus we see as proof of God's will for the world, and in the Paschal Mystery the demonstration of the cycle of struggle.

It is true that the Jesus who lives in us died but did not die. But just as true is the fact that we have all known resurrection in our own lives as well. We have been crucified, each of us, one way or another, and been raised up again. What had been bad for us at the time, we now see, was in the end an invitation to rise to new life. The invitation was to a road, we now admit, which we would never have taken ourselves if we had not been forced to travel it. Looking back we know now that this hard road was really the journey that brought us at least one step closer to wholeness in a world in which wholeness can never exist. It may be precisely because we lust after some kind of mythical wholeness that we fail to see the life-giving truths that come to us one byway, one fragment at a time.

Hope is not some kind of delusional optimism to be resorted to because we simply cannot face the hard facts that threaten to swamp our hearts. People do die and leave us. Friends do leave and desert us. Businesses do crumble and destroy us financially. Loves do dry up and disappear. Desires do come to dust. Careers do come to ruin. Disease does debilitate us. Evil does exist. But through it all, hope remains, nevertheless, a choice.

Hope rides on the decision either to believe that God stands on this dark road waiting to walk with us toward new light again or to despair of the fact that God who is faithful is eternally faithful and will sustain us in our darkness one more time. We can begin to build a new life when death comes. We can reach out to make friends with others rather than curl up, hurt and angry, waiting for someone to come to us. We can allow ourselves to love again, knowing now that love is a prize that comes in many shapes and forms. We can allow ourselves to cultivate new joys, new interests. We can take the experiences of the past and use them to mine a new life lode. We can give ourselves over to resisting what must be resisted whether we ever live to see it expelled or not. We can let go of a finished present so that what is about to happen in the future can begin. We can decide to go through life with open hands rather than to trap ourselves inside a heart closed to everything but the past.

Hope and despair are not opposites. They are cut from the very same cloth, made from the very same material, shaped from the very same circumstances. Every life finds itself forced to choose one from the other, one day at a time, one circumstance after another. The sunflower, that plant which in shadow turns its head relentlessly toward the sun, is the patron saint of those in despair. When darkness descends on the soul, it is time, like the sunflower, to go looking for whatever good thing in life there is that can bring us comfort. Then we need music and hobbies and friends and fun and new thought — not alcohol and wild nights and immersion in the pain that is killing us. The worst thing is to dull rather than displace the pain with the kind of joy or comfort that makes us new. "Give light," Erasmus wrote, "and the darkness will disappear of itself."

The only difference between hope and despair is that despair shapes an attitude of mind. Hope creates a quality of soul. The Irish love to tell the story of Paddy McGarrity, who spent his life bemoaning all the circumstances of his life. Nothing satisfied him. But one particularly gracious summer day the sun burst out through the fog and rain of the country and spread over the Irish hills in a blaze of glory. Surely even Paddy would see the beauty of life in this! "Ho, Paddy," the parish priest called to him over the fence. "Isn't it a beautiful day!" "Ah, sure, Father," Paddy moaned, "but will it *last?*"

Despair colors the way we look at things, makes us suspicious of the future, makes us negative about the present. Most of all, despair leads us to ignore the very possibilities that could save us, or worse, leads us to want to hurt as we have been hurt ourselves.

Hope, on the other hand, takes life on its own terms, knows that whatever happens God lives in it, and expects that, whatever its twists and turns, it will ultimately yield its good to those who live it consciously, to those who live it to the hilt.

When tragedy strikes, when trouble comes, when life disappoints us, we stand at the crossroads between hope and despair, torn and hurting. Despair cements us in the present. Hope sends us dancing around dark corners trusting in a tomorrow we cannot see because of the multiple pasts of life which we cannot forget. Despair says that there is no place to go but here.

When I say that I am in despair, I am really saying that I have given up on God. Despair says that I am God and if I can't do anything about this situation, then nothing and nobody can.

Despair is the affliction of the small-minded who have not so much lost their faith as they have lost their memory. Hope says, remember where you have been before and know that God is waiting for you someplace else now, to go on again to something new.

Life is not one road. It is many roads, the walking of which provides the raw material out of which we find hope in the midst of despair. Every dimension of the process of struggle is a call to draw from a well of new understandings. It is in these understandings that hope dwells. It is that wisdom that carries us beyond the dark night of struggle to the dawn of new wisdom and new strength.

24. Hope: The Resurrection of the Spirit

❦

It's hard to imagine a bleaker place on earth than Bosnia in 1992. Ethnic tensions, centuries old, had flared again in the ancient region. Protestant Serbs, Orthodox Croats, and Sunni Muslims battled for national political control under the banner of religious freedom, long established, and ethnic identity, long defined. Detention camps given to inhumane treatment, brutal torture, and ethnic cleansing flourished in every segment of the population while one group tried to contain the others. One segment of the society drove the others out of regions that had been integrated for years. Neighbors forced neighbors from family homes and homesteads generations old. A history of bitterness long thought gone raged again and deepened. Hope for any kind of peaceful coexistence ebbed by the day. The fighting was hand to hand, street to street, man to man. It was a bloody, hopeless time.

Vedran Smailovic was a Bosnian. He had been born, in fact, on November 11, 1956, right in the heart of Sarajevo. The fourth of five children in a highly musical family, Vedran himself became a professional musician, a cellist who played everything from symphonies and chamber music to folk and pop.

By the age of thirty-seven Vedran was the principal cellist of the prestigious Sarajevo Opera Theater. Looking back on that period years later, Smailovic described the city in those days as "the capital of hell." The Opera Theater lay destroyed. The economy had been shattered. The prospect of ever reuniting the country again dwindled by the day. The very definition of "human" was in question.

Then, at 4:00 p.m. on May 27, 1992, a long line of starving, helpless people were shelled as they waited in front of the only bakery in Sarajevo that still had enough flour to make bread. Twenty-two people died in the attack as Vedran Smailovic stood at his apartment building window a hundred yards away and watched it happen.

The next day, as hungry people lined up again to beg for bread — certain that they would die if they didn't come to the bakery again and well aware they could die if they did — Vedran Smailovic, dressed in the black suit and tie in which he had played every night until the Opera Theater was destroyed, arrived carrying his cello and a chair.

Smailovic sat down in the rubble in the square and, surrounded by debris and the remnants of death and the despair of the living, began to play Albinoni's mournful "Adagio." And, whatever the continuing danger, he came back to the square every day after that for twenty-one days to do the same. Over and over again, the "Adagio" sounded the memory that there are some things in the human enterprise that simply cannot be suppressed.

Today in the place where he sat there is a monument of a man in a chair playing a cello. But the monument is not to Smailovic's music. It is to his refusal to surrender the hope that beauty could be reborn in the midst of a living hell.

Even more important, perhaps, is the fact that that small sound of hope rings on around the world. Smailovic was called to play the "Adagio" in Seattle; in Washington, D. C., during the inaugural celebrations of President Clinton; at the Cathedral of St. John the Divine in New York City; at the Statue of Liberty in commemoration of the thousandth day of the siege of Sarajevo; and in 1998 in Belfast prior to the signing of the peace accord in Northern Ireland. Finally, the renowned cellist Yo-Yo Ma played David Wilde's "The Cellist of Sarajevo" at the International Cello Festival in Manchester, England, in 1994 with Smailovic in attendance. Clearly, hope is a spark that once struck will simply not be extinguished.

The story is Smailovic's story, yes. But it is also the story of every human being who has been to the underworld of life and risen again. It is the story of those who, like Jacob, have wrestled with God and prevailed — hung on, stayed the course, dug down deep into their souls and found life where no life seemed able to exist. That is the task of hope in the face of despair: to find out how much life we can still make with whatever of it we have left.

Life is an exercise in twists and turns of the unpredictable and the unsought. The Shakers remind us in their classic hymn that "to turn, and to turn" is part of the discipline of "coming round right." Jacob did not defeat his opponent. He simply survived the struggle. I never wrote fiction but I did go on writing. We become what we are, in other words, but we do not do it, in most cases, in any kind of linear progression. We go from one struggle to another, becoming as we go.

The hard thing to come to understand in life is that it is the becoming that counts, not the achievements, not the roles in which we manage to mantle ourselves. But becoming is our most byzantine task. Giving ourselves over to be sculpted can take a lifetime of shifts and gyrations, of aimless orbits and dizzying spins, of near despair and of dogged, intransigent, tenacious hope. "Turn your face to the sun and the shadows fall always behind you," the native people of New Zealand say. When despair comes, in other words, in order to dispel it with hope, we have to make the effort.

Hope is not a matter of waiting for things outside us to get better. It is about getting better inside about what is going on inside. It is about becoming open to the God of newness. It is about allowing ourselves to let go of the present, to believe in the future we cannot see but can trust to God. Surrendering to the demands of the moment, holding on when holding on seems pointless, brings us to that point of personal transformation which is the juncture of maturity and sagacity. Then, whatever the circumstances, however hard the task, the struggles of life may indeed shunt us from mountaintop to mountaintop but they will not destroy us.

We always think of hope as grounded in the future. That's wrong, I think. Hope is fulfilled in the future but it depends on our ability to remember that, like Jacob, we have survived everything in life to this point — and have emerged in even better form than we were when those troubles began. So why not this latest situation, too? Then we hope because we have no reason not to hope. Hope is what sits by a window and waits for one more dawn, despite the fact that there isn't an ounce of proof in tonight's black, black sky that it can possibly come.

Despair is more likely a spiritual state than a psychological one, more sure to be a subjective one than a medical one. It doesn't rest in our genes; it rests in our valuation of life, of God, of the homing instincts of the self. It burns out under the grace of certain belief in the ultimate goodness of God who is here but not visible, present but not controlling, the one permanence in our changing lives. Hope is the last great gift to rise out of the grave of despair.